Dear Jorge,

This book is a gift of love and imagination. May each page be an invitation to explore new worlds, discover exciting adventures, and dream big. May the magic of stories always accompany you, just as you brighten our lives with your smile. With all my affection, I dedicate these words to you, my dear son.

With love, Mom.

Yasmim Lima

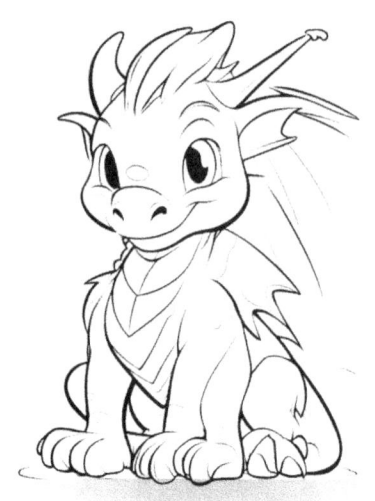

This Book Belongs to:

_____

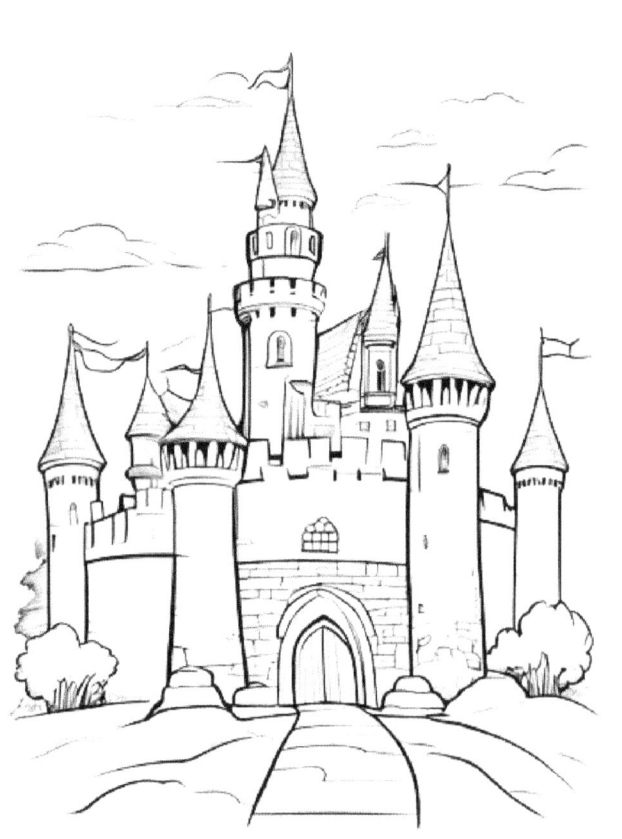
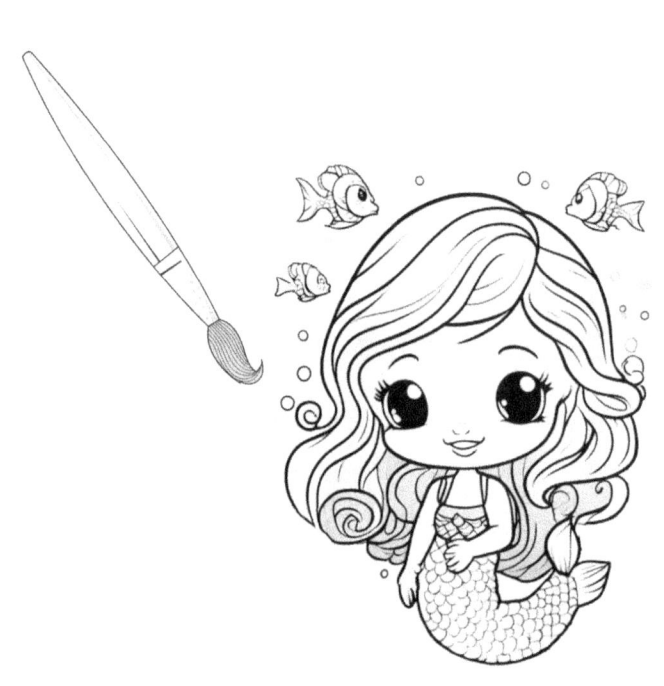

ALL RIGHTS RESERVED©

No part of this publication may be reproduced, distributed, or transmitted in any form or by any means, including photocopying, recording, or other electronic or mechanical methods, without the prior written permission of the publisher, except for brief quotations incorporated in critical reviews and other specific noncommercial uses. Any unauthorized replica of this work is prohibited.

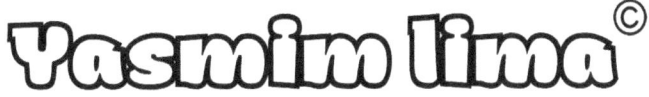

Test Color Page

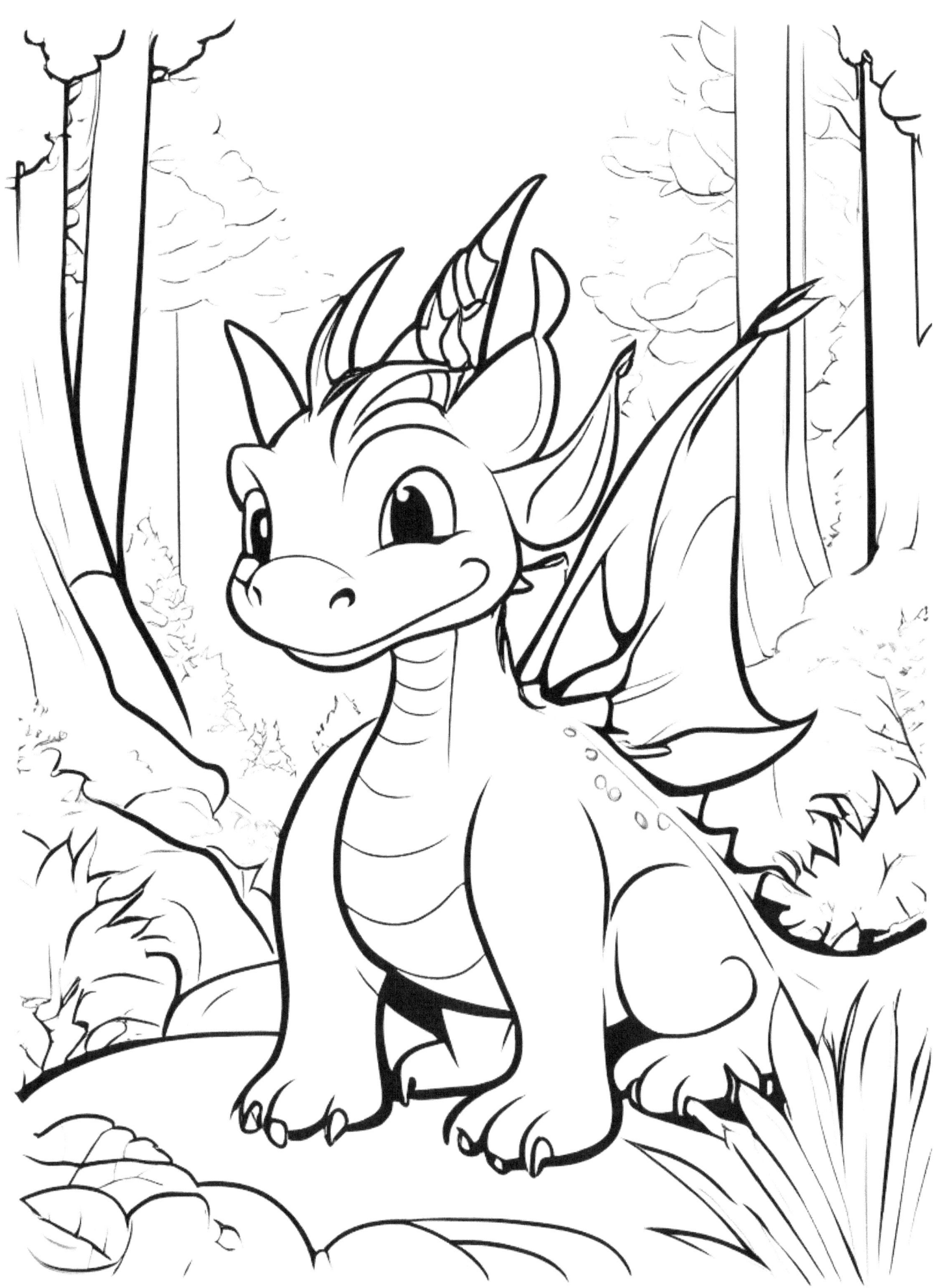

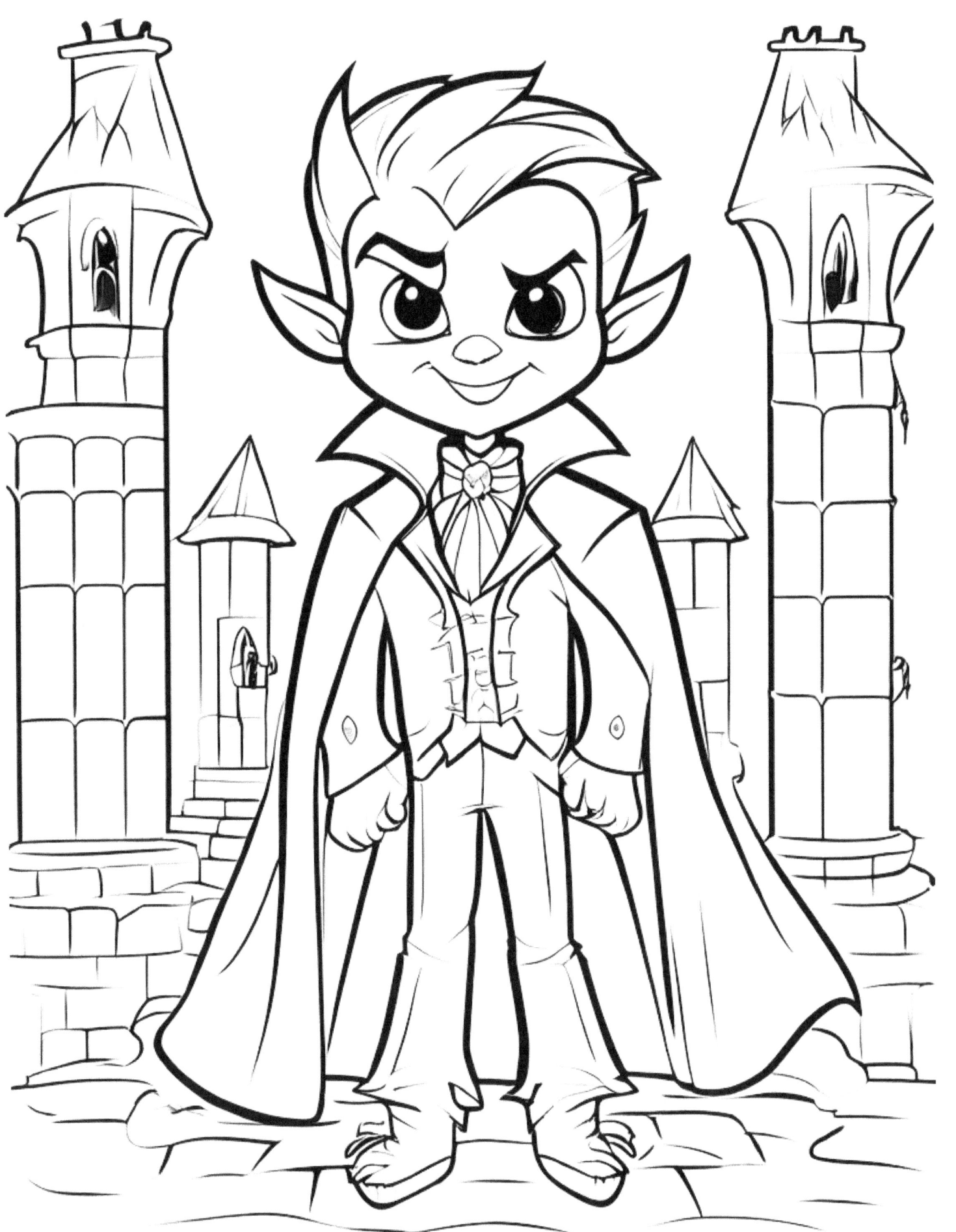

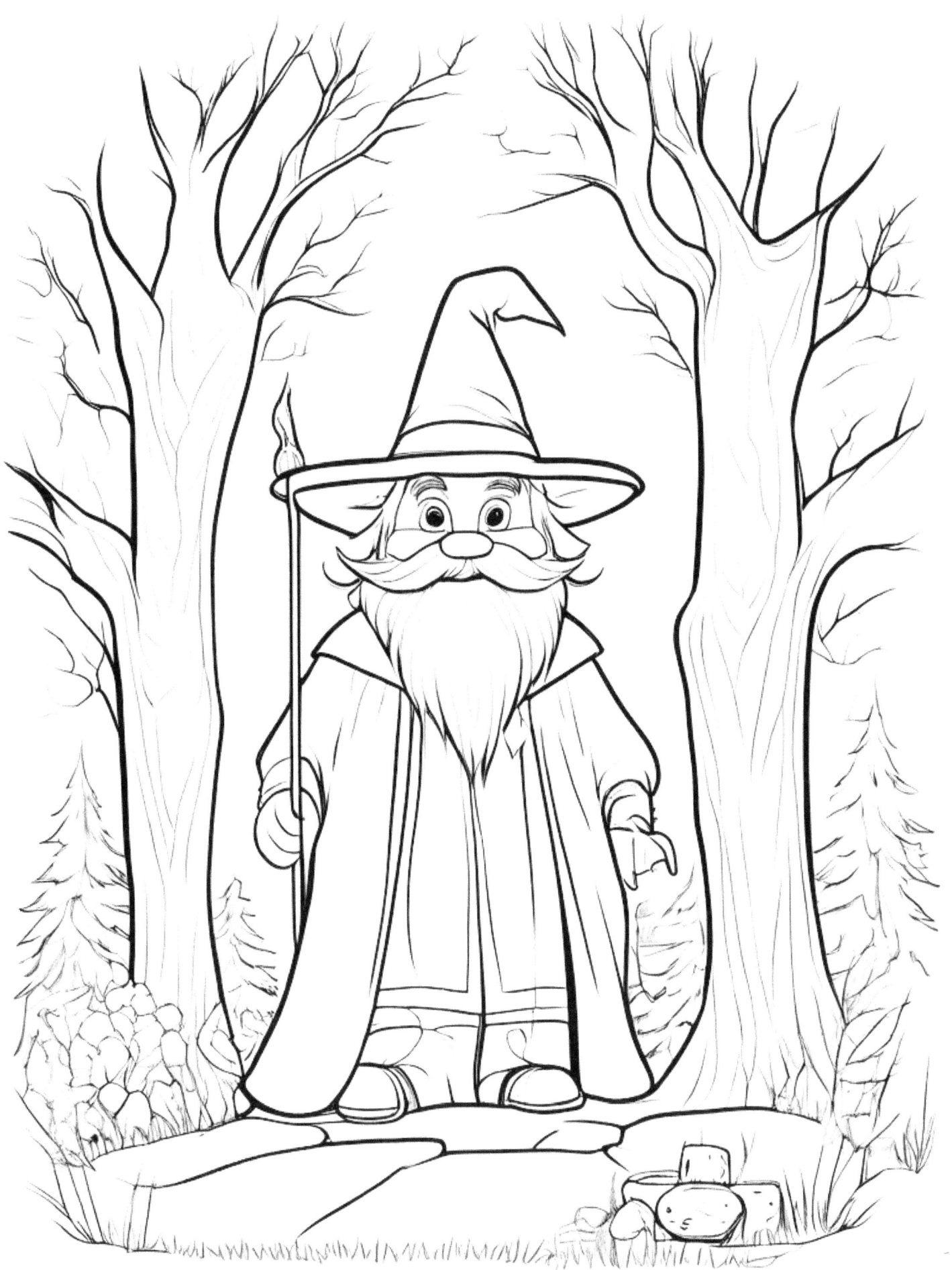

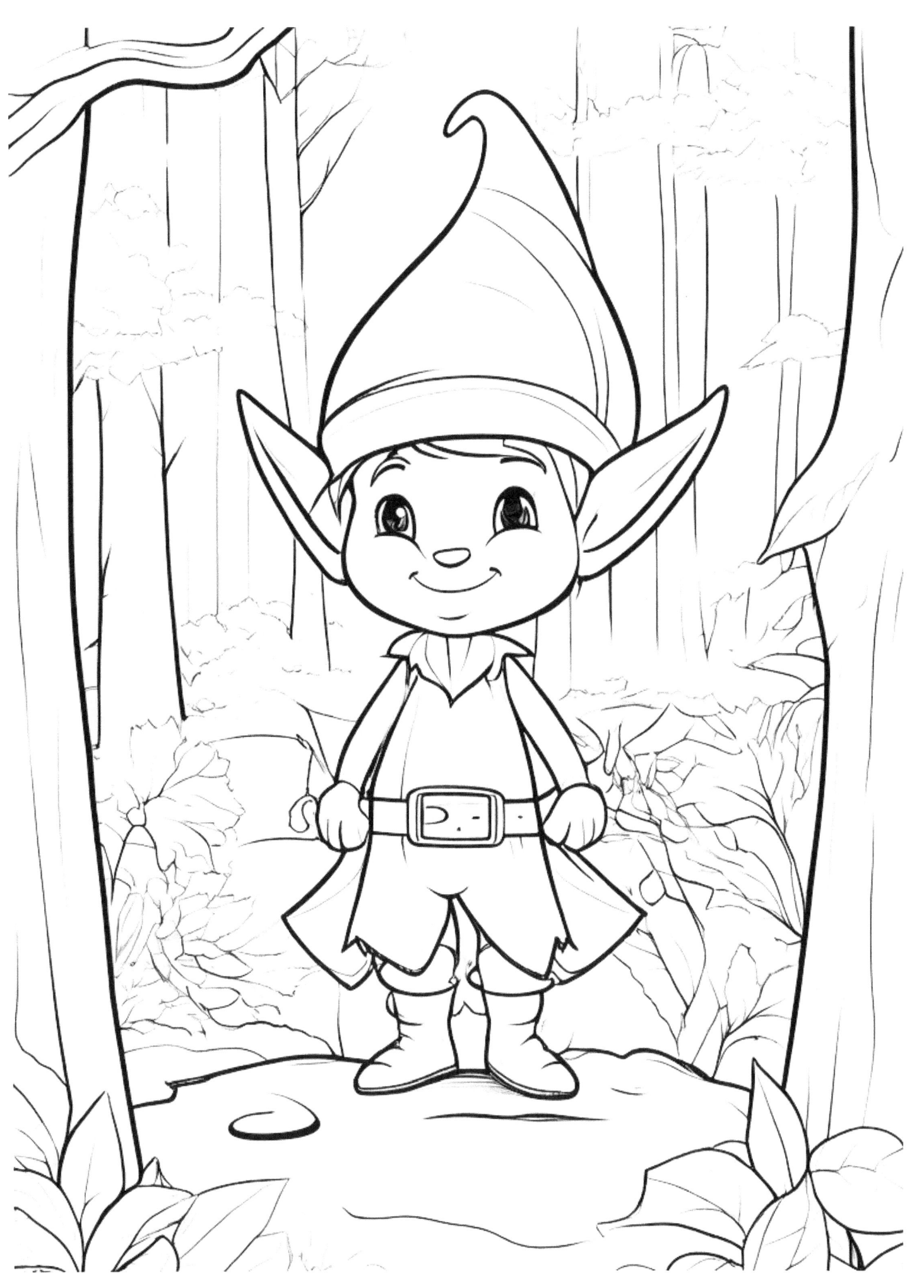

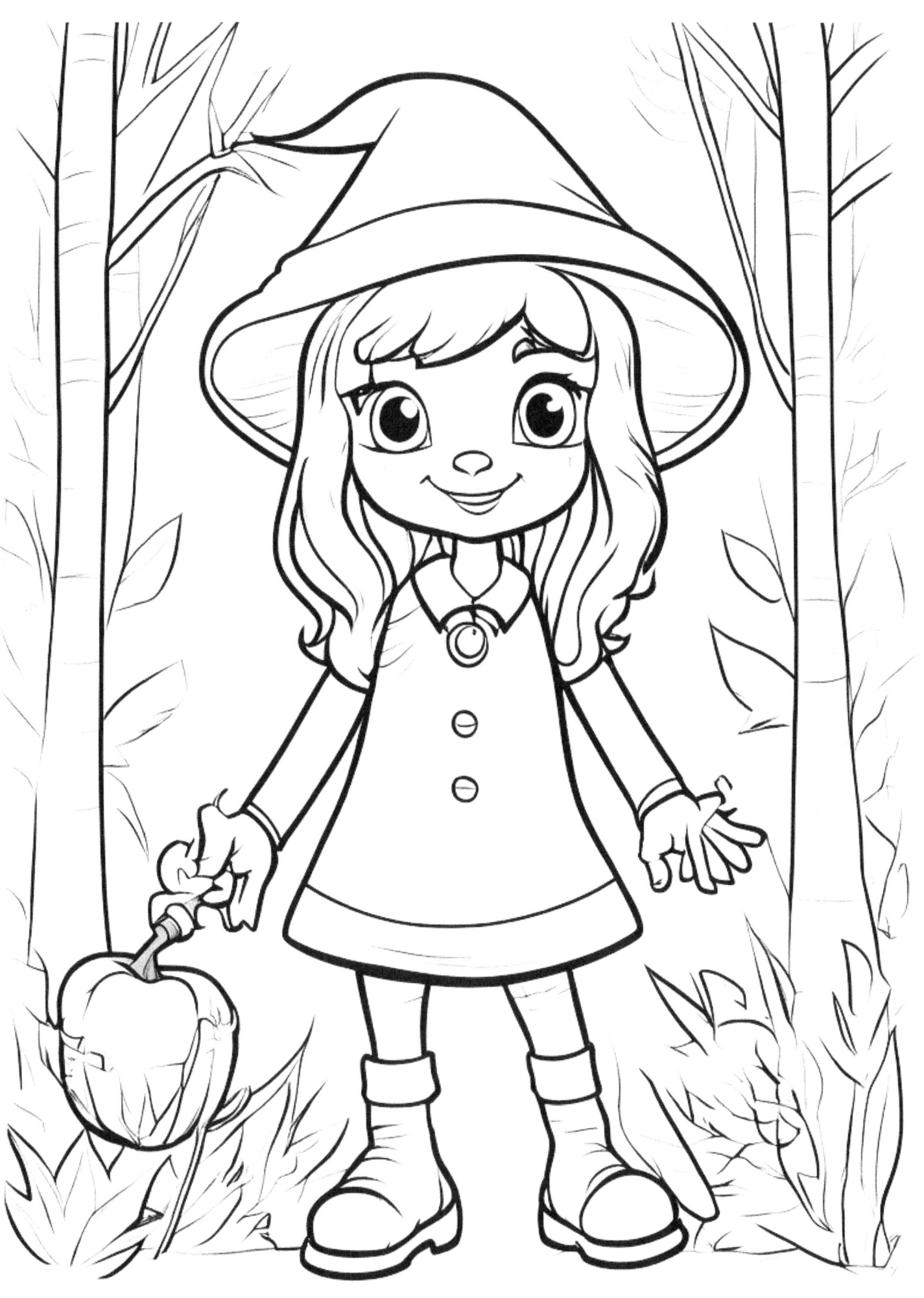

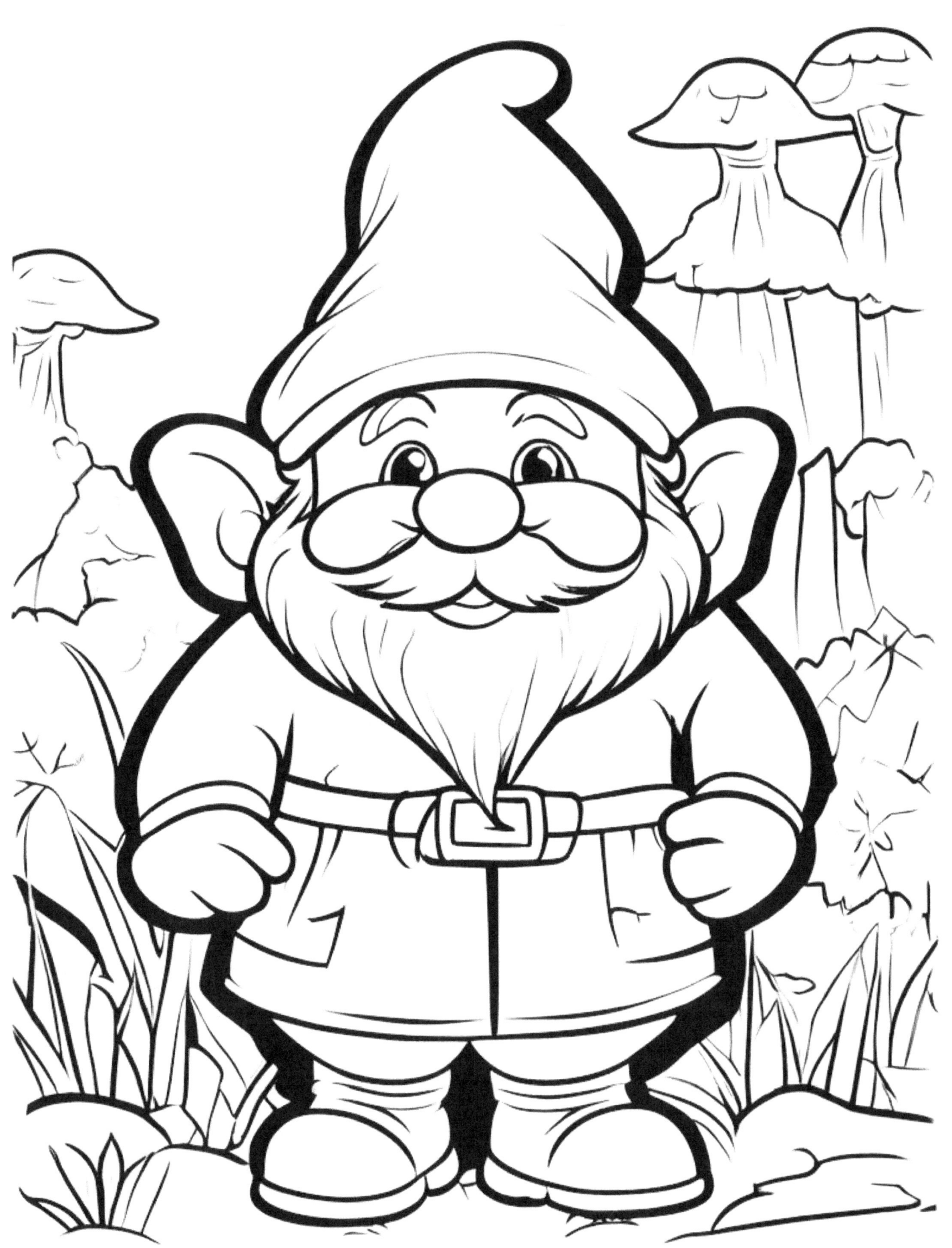

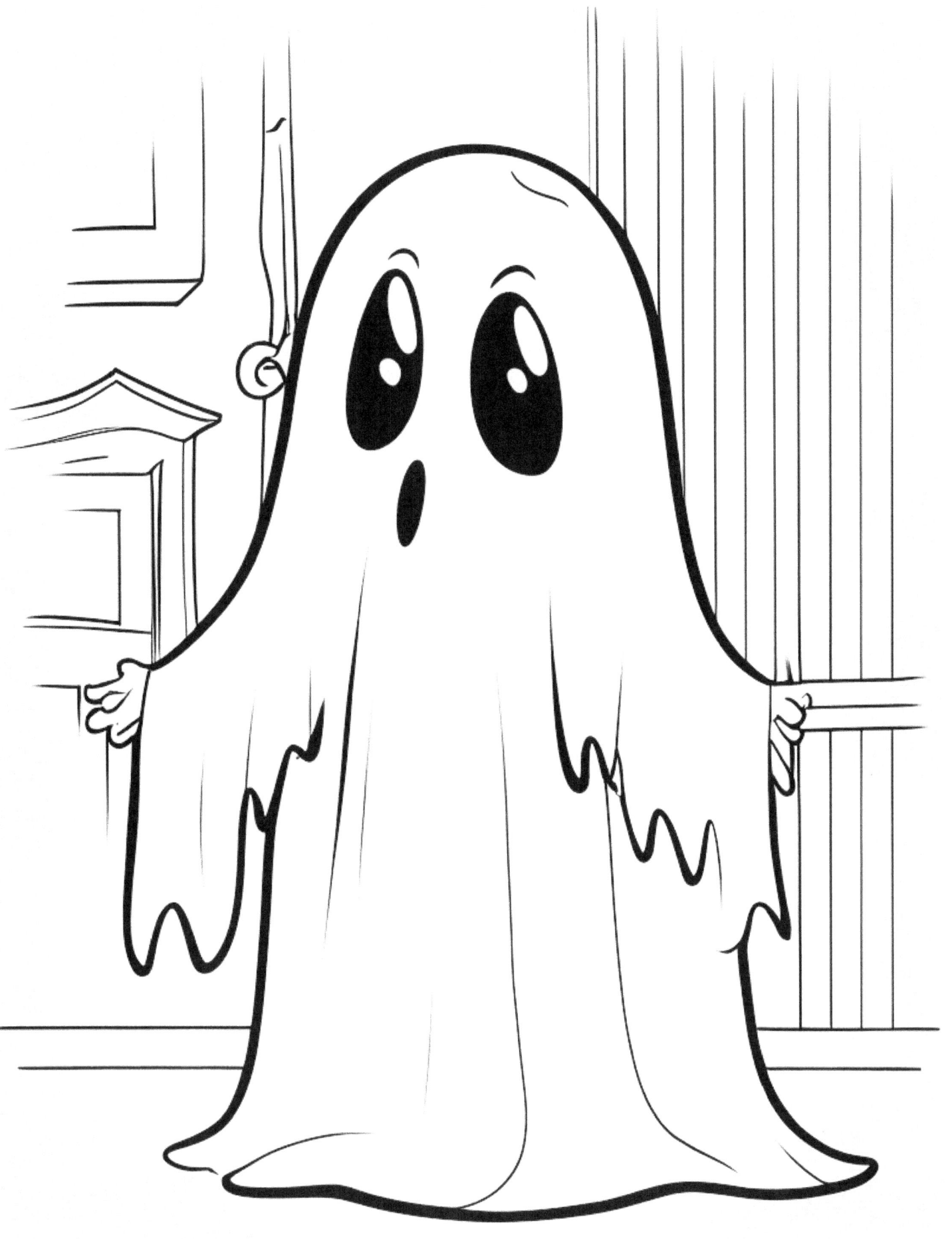

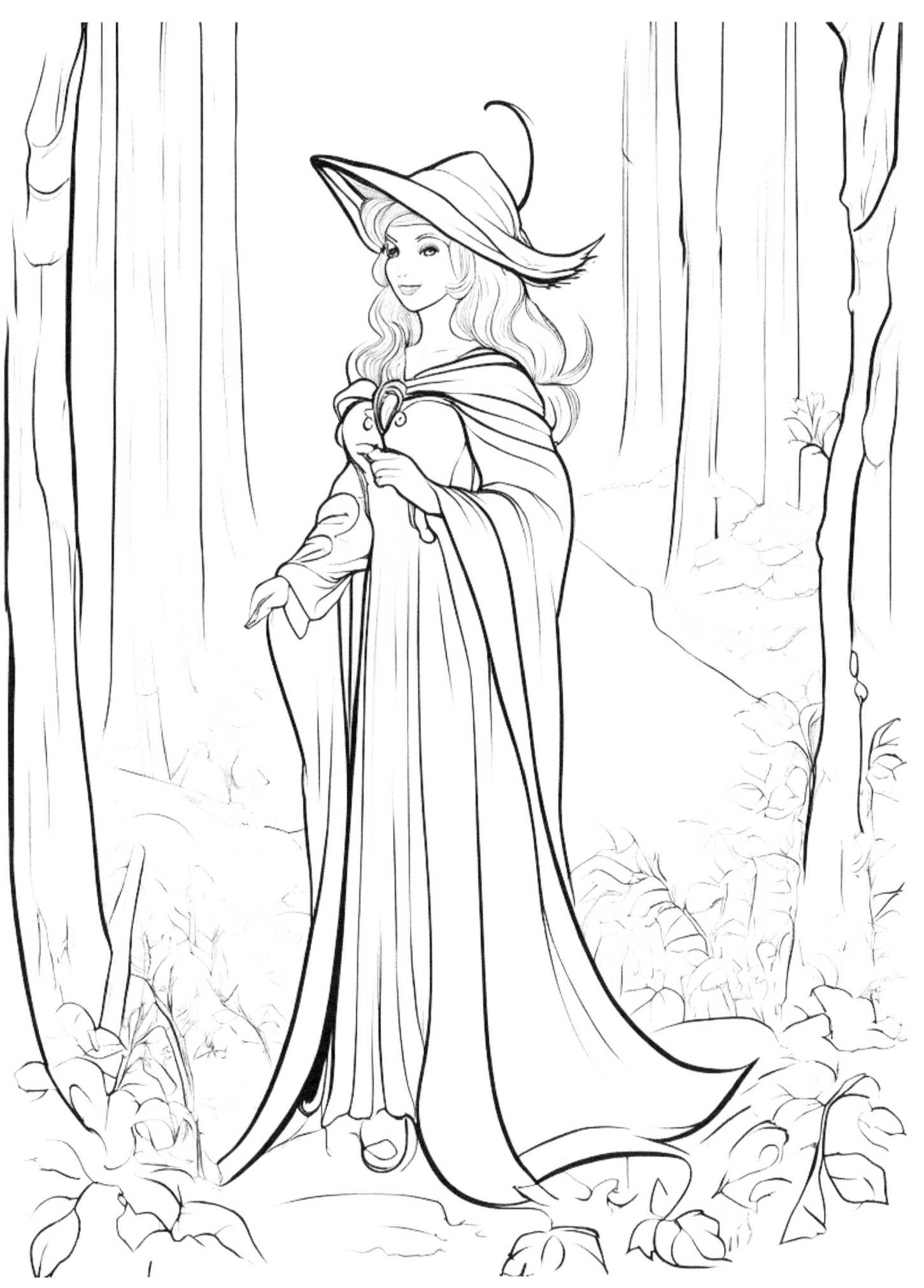

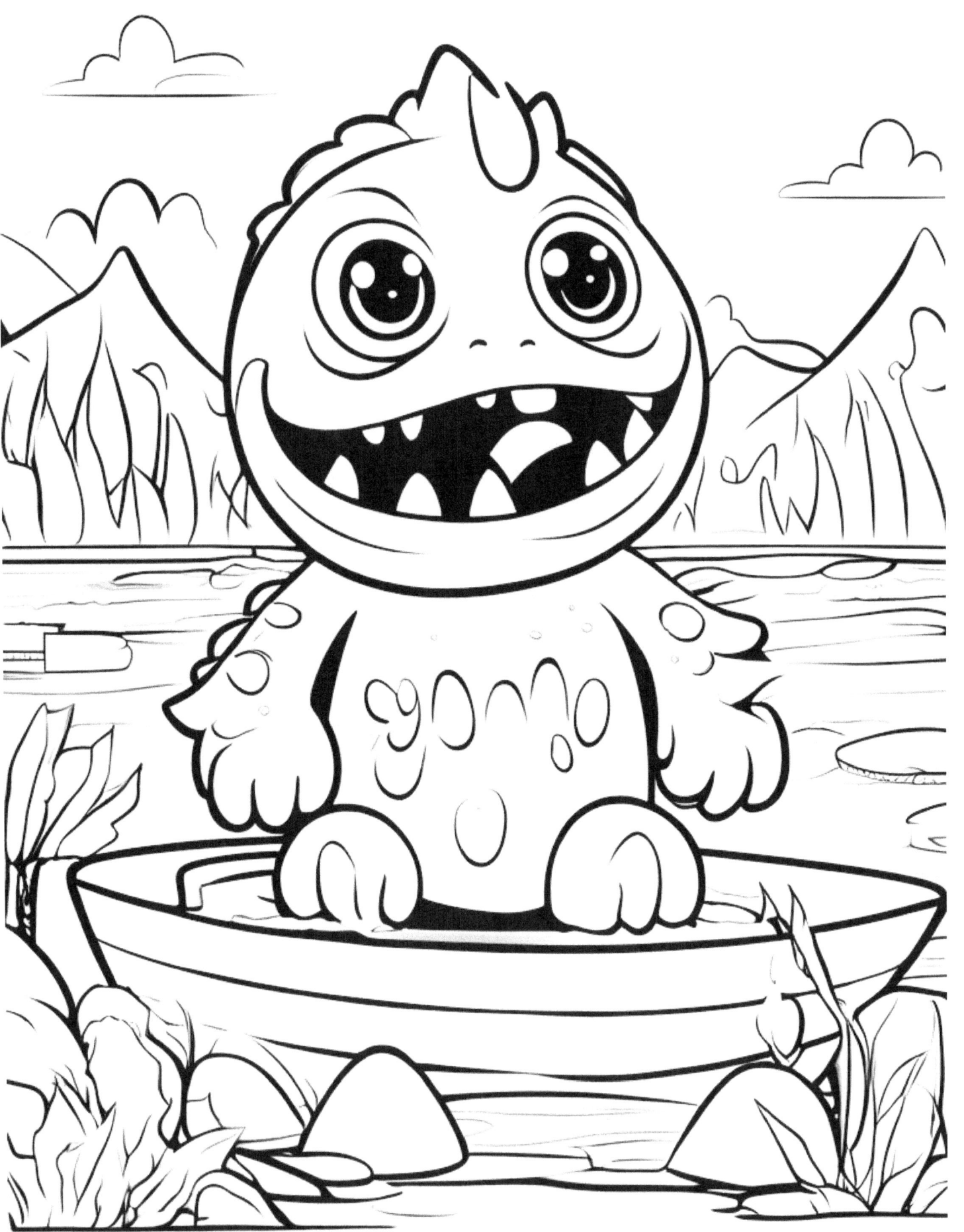

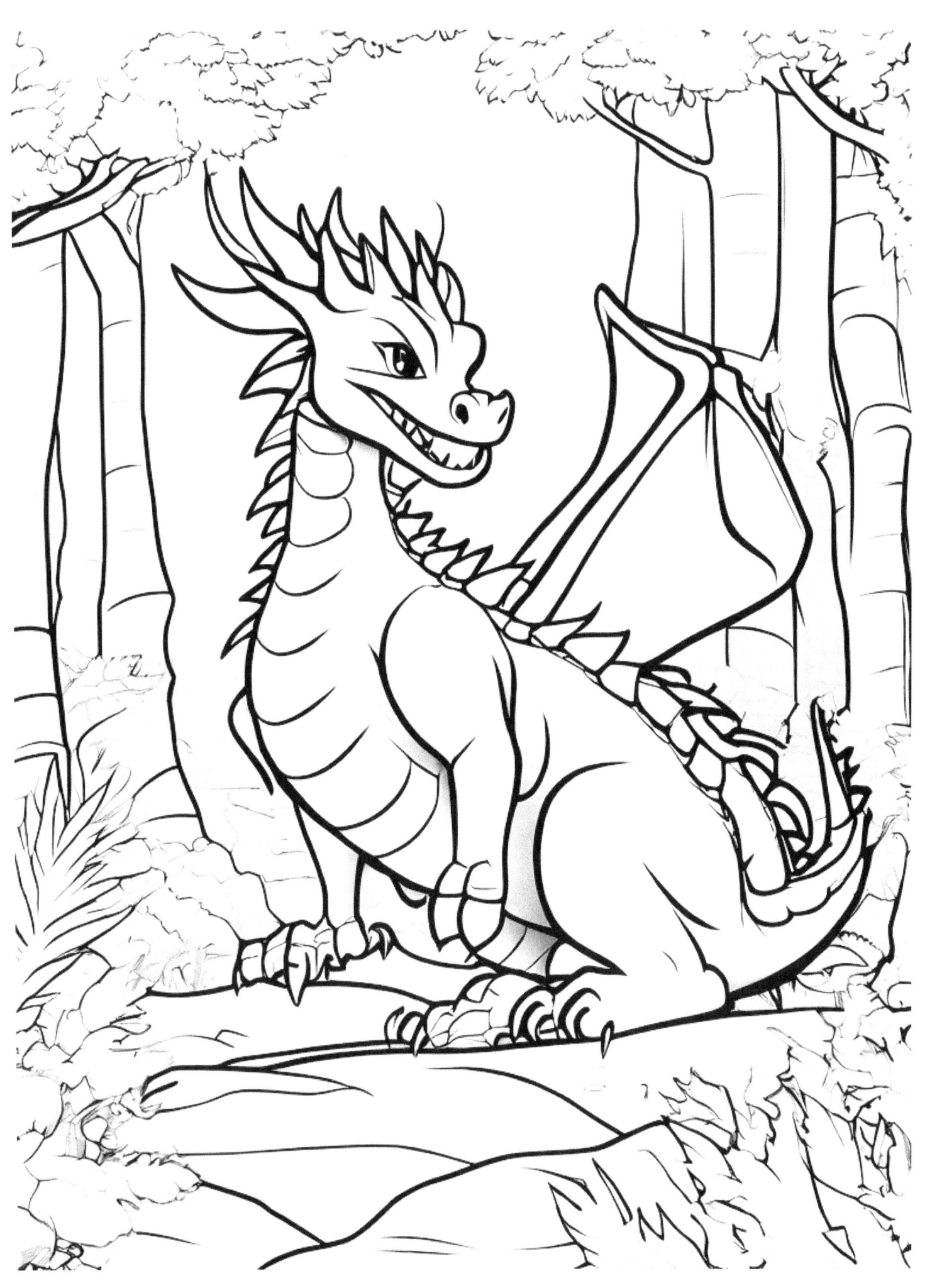

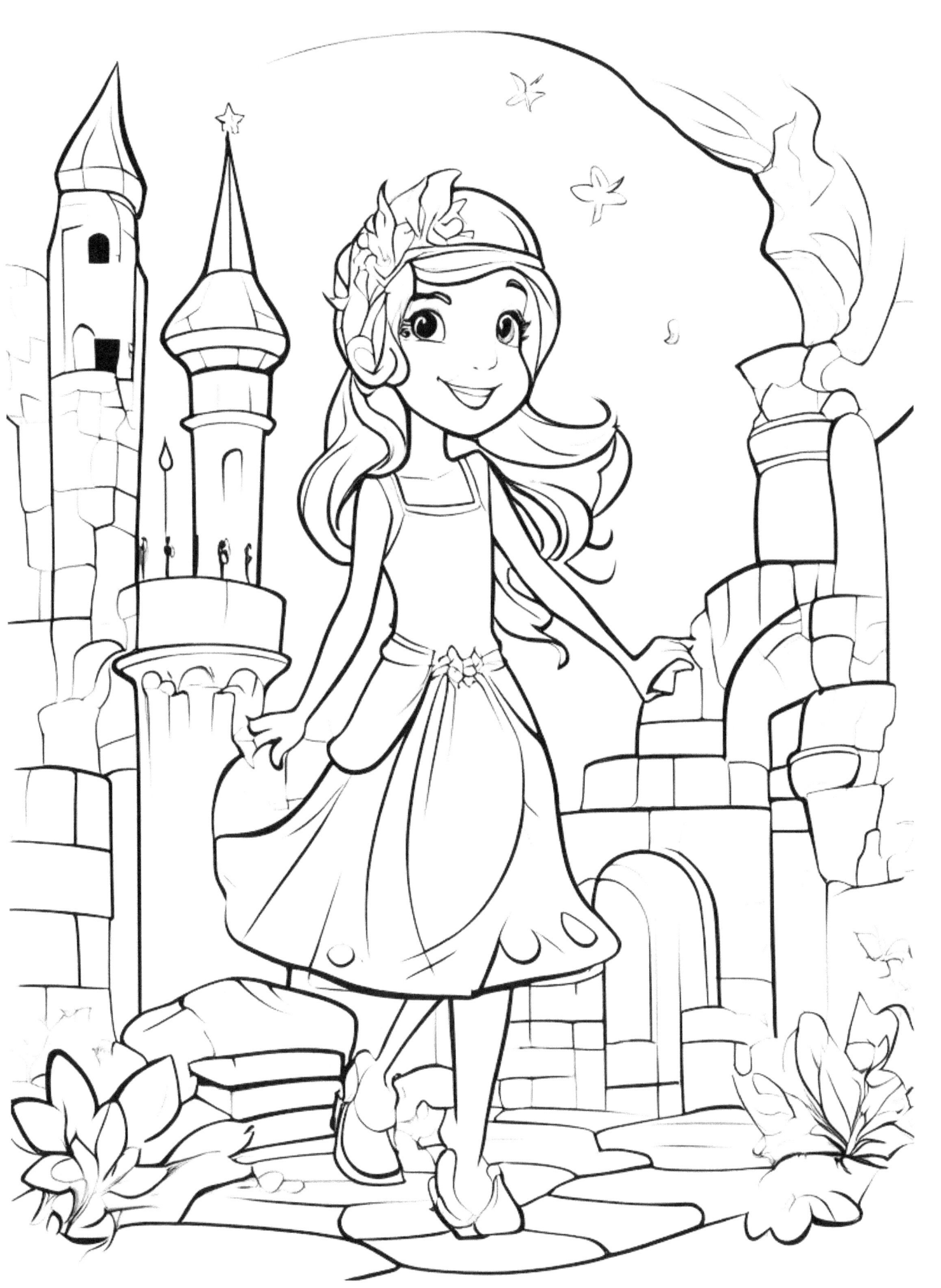

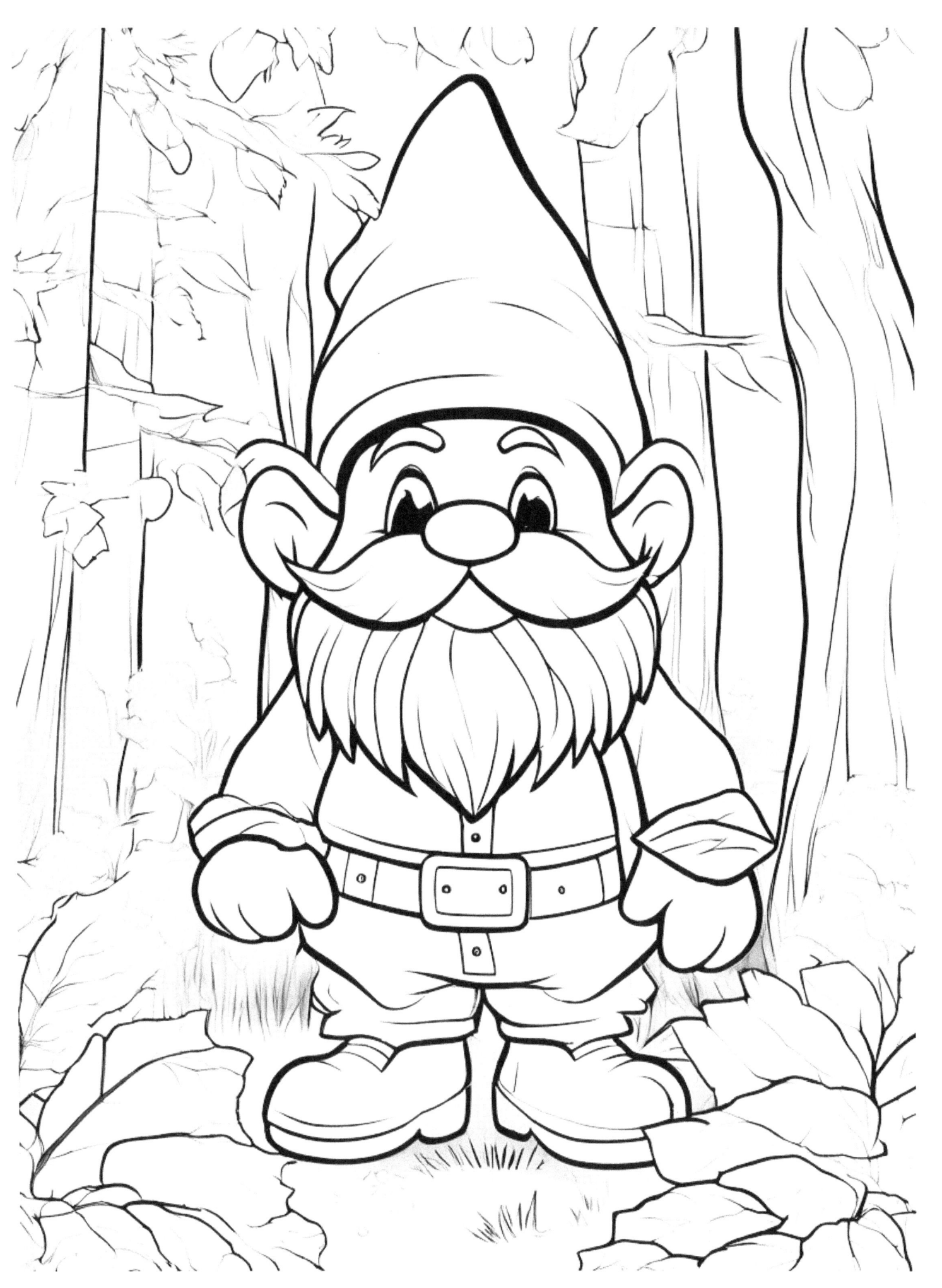

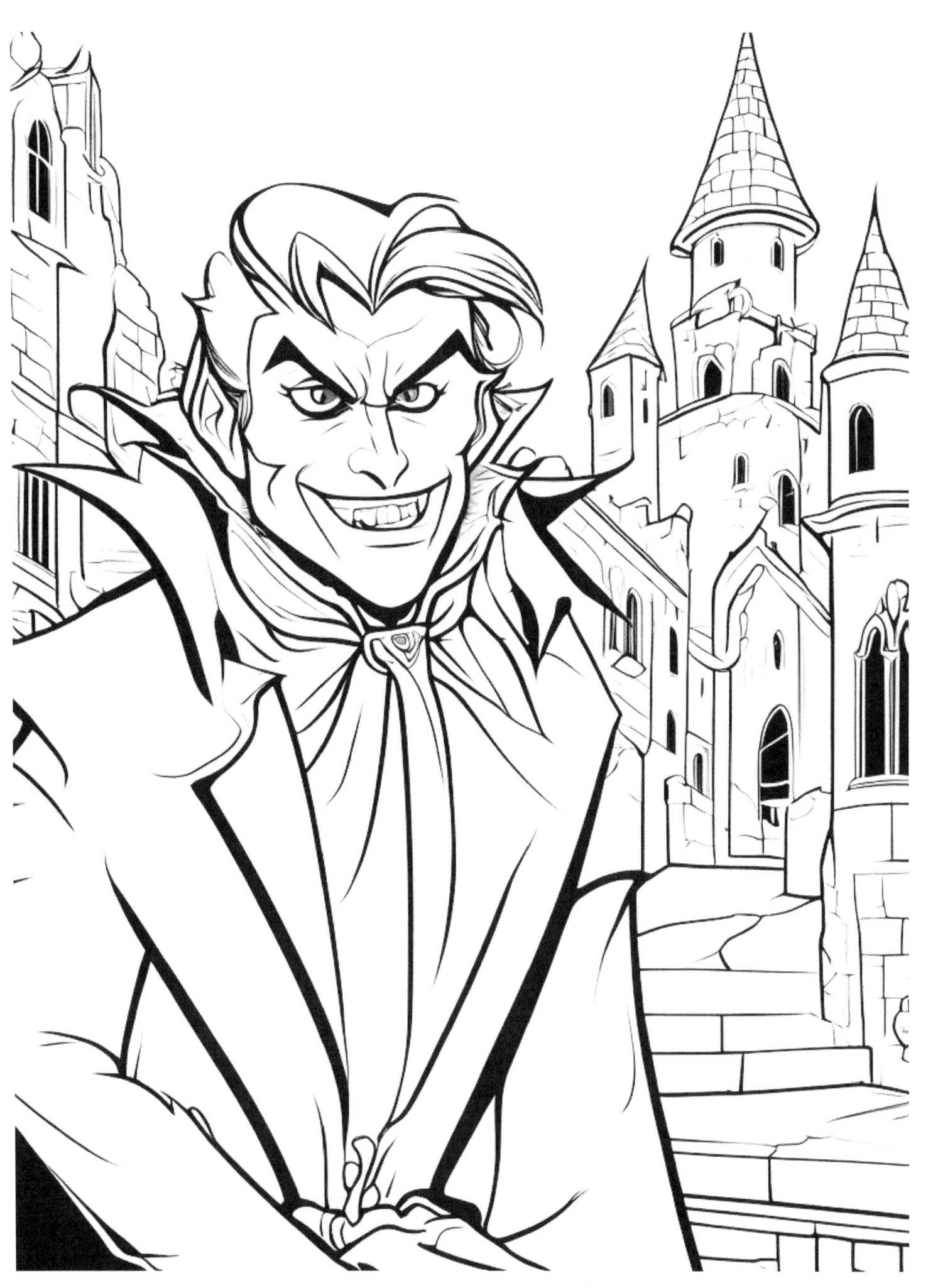

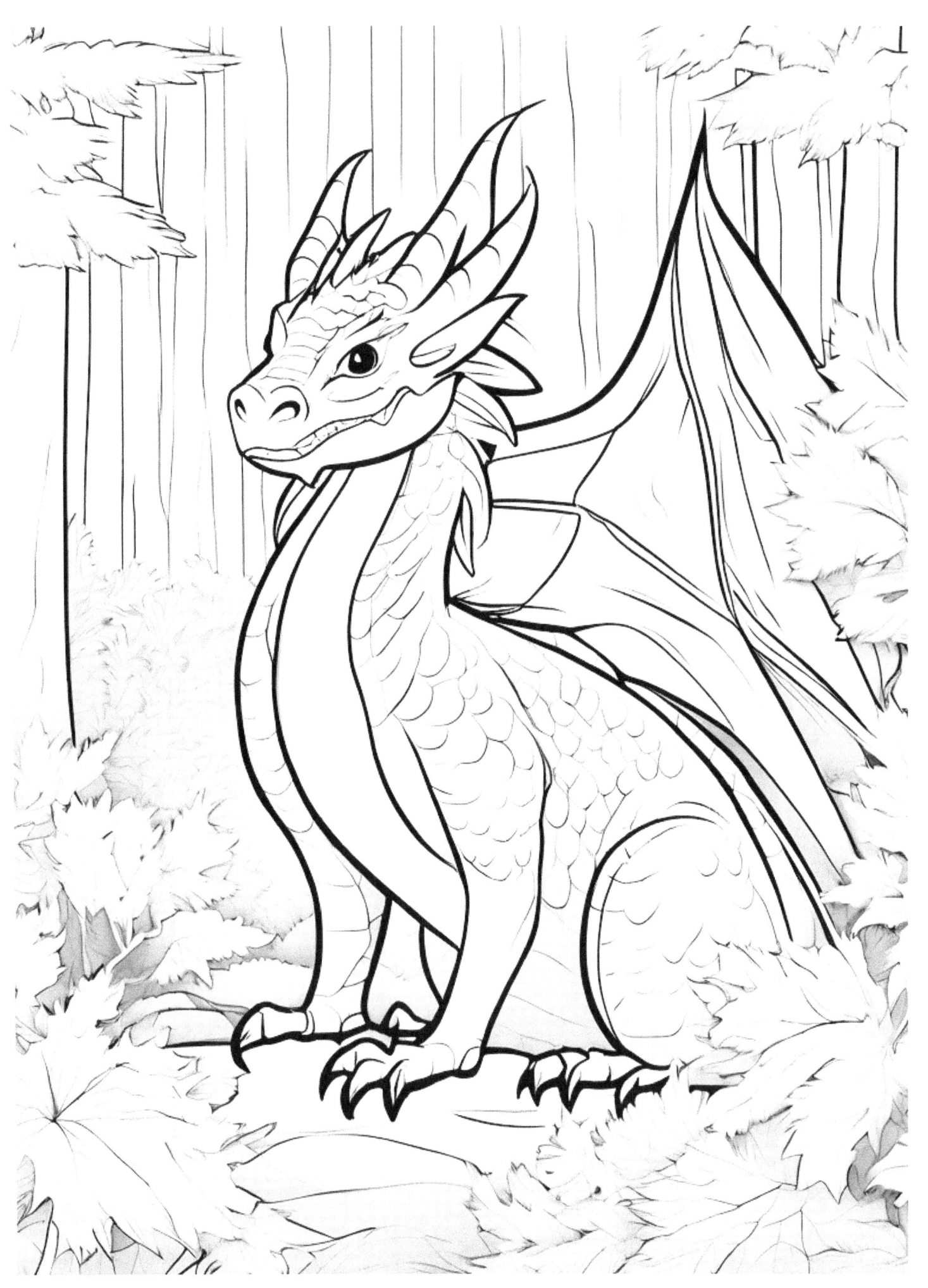

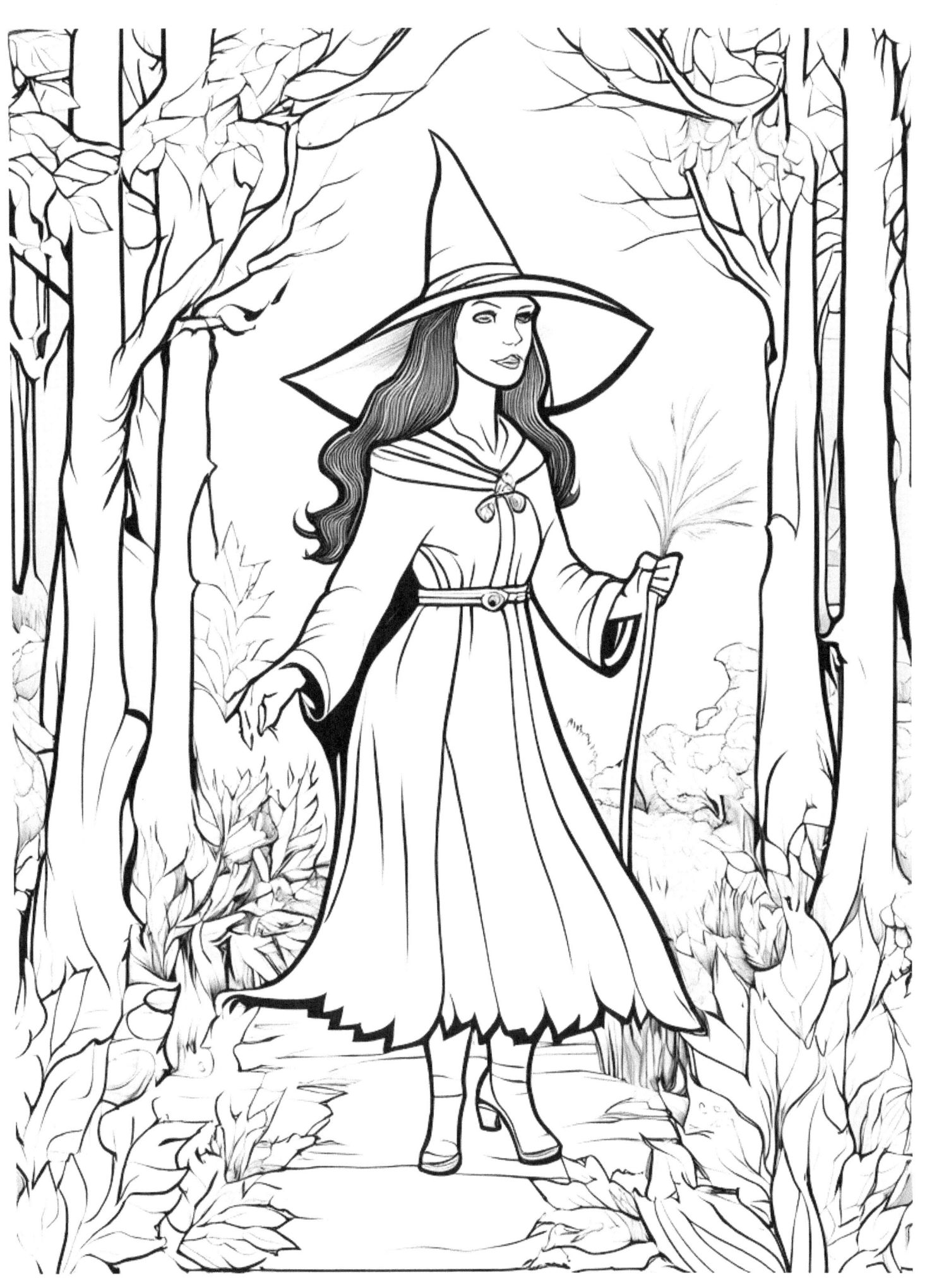

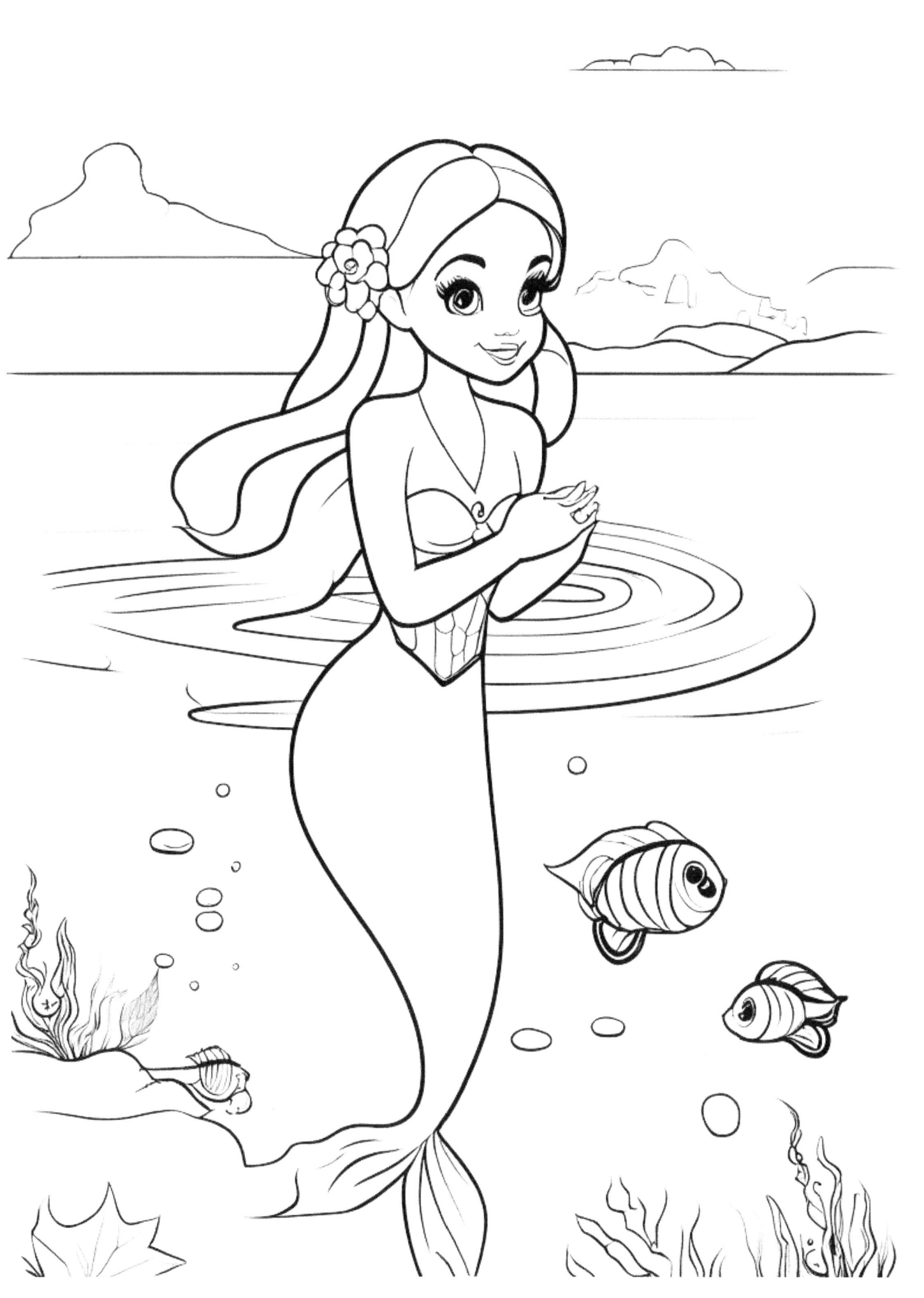

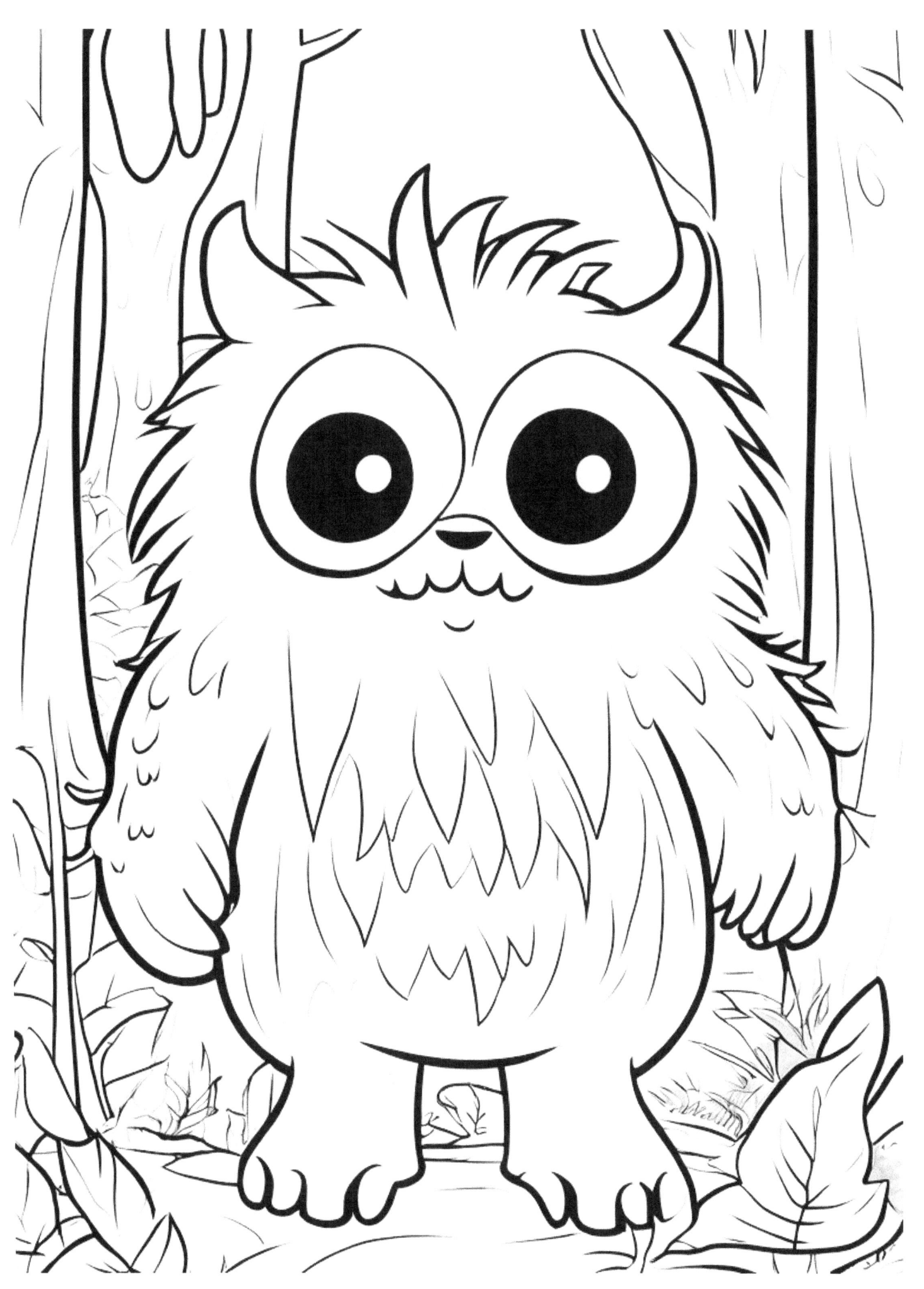

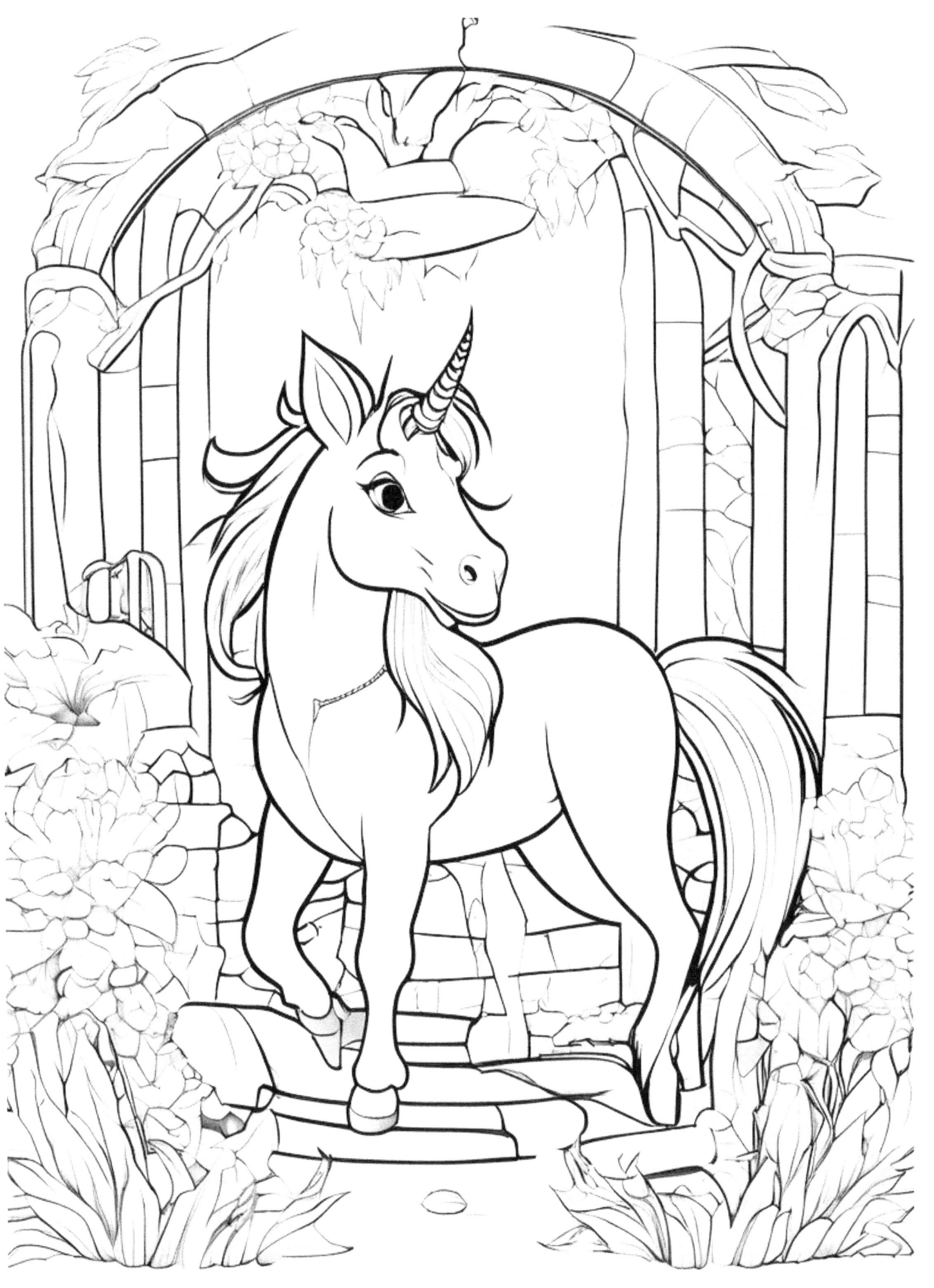

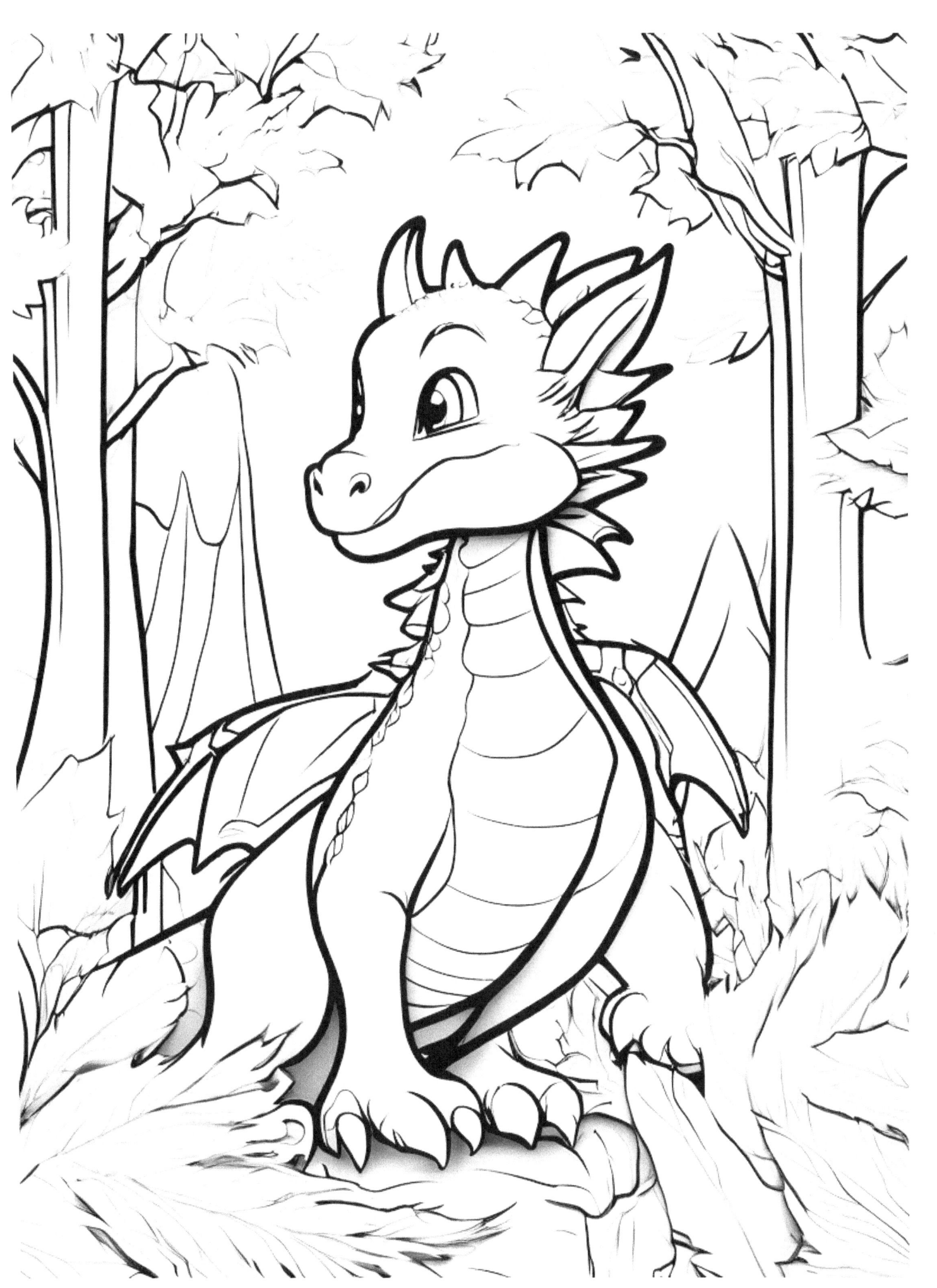

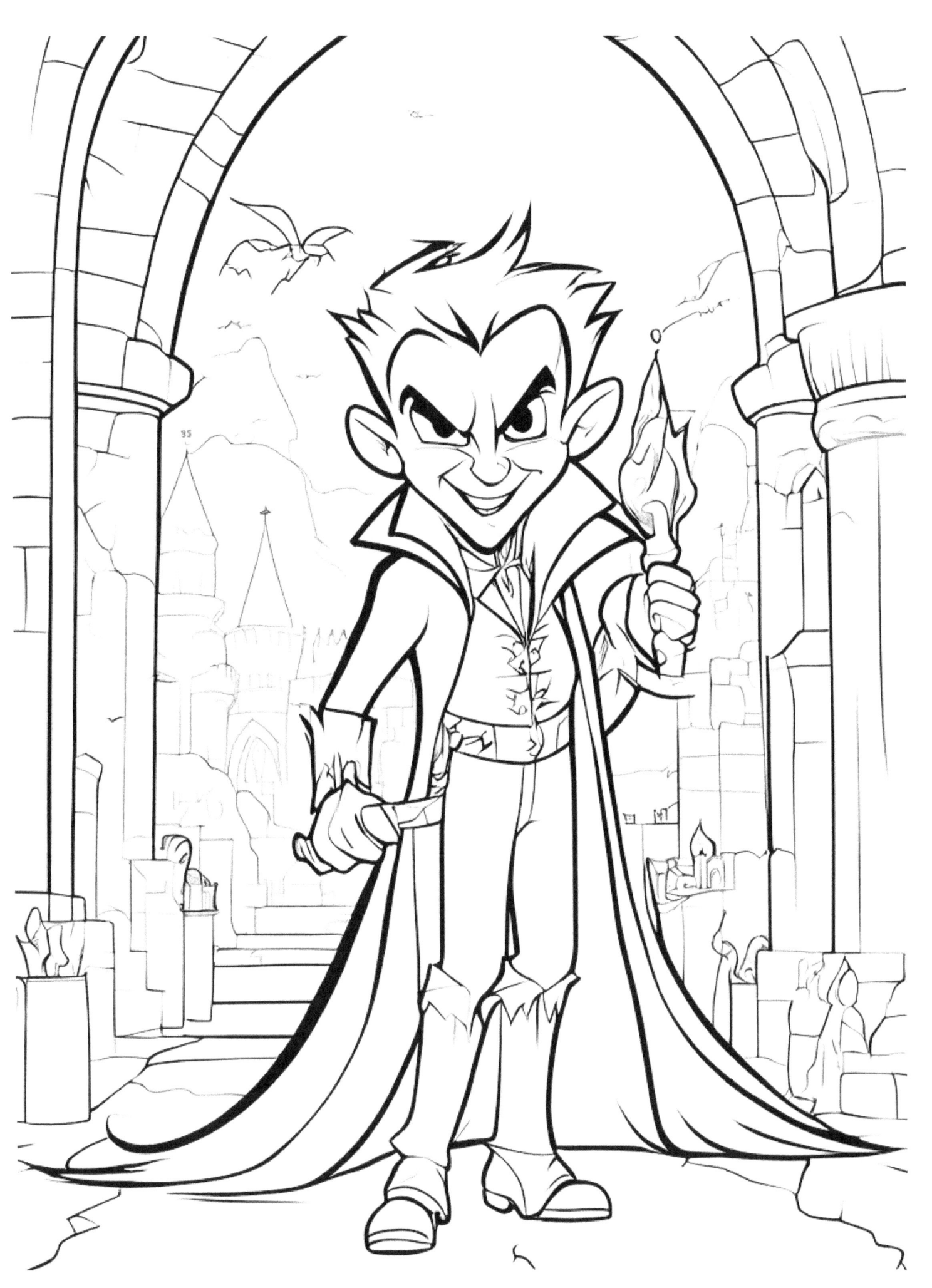

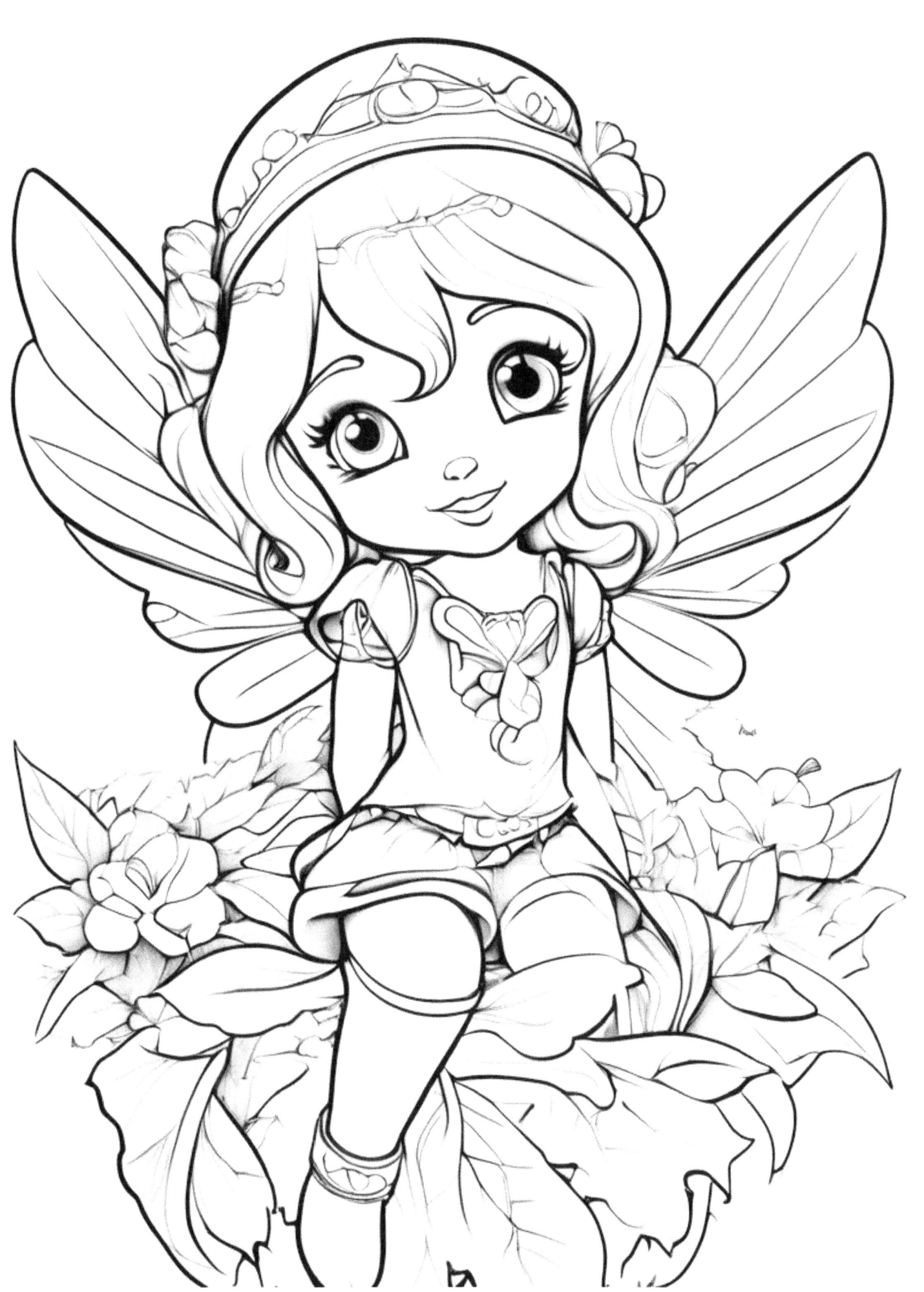

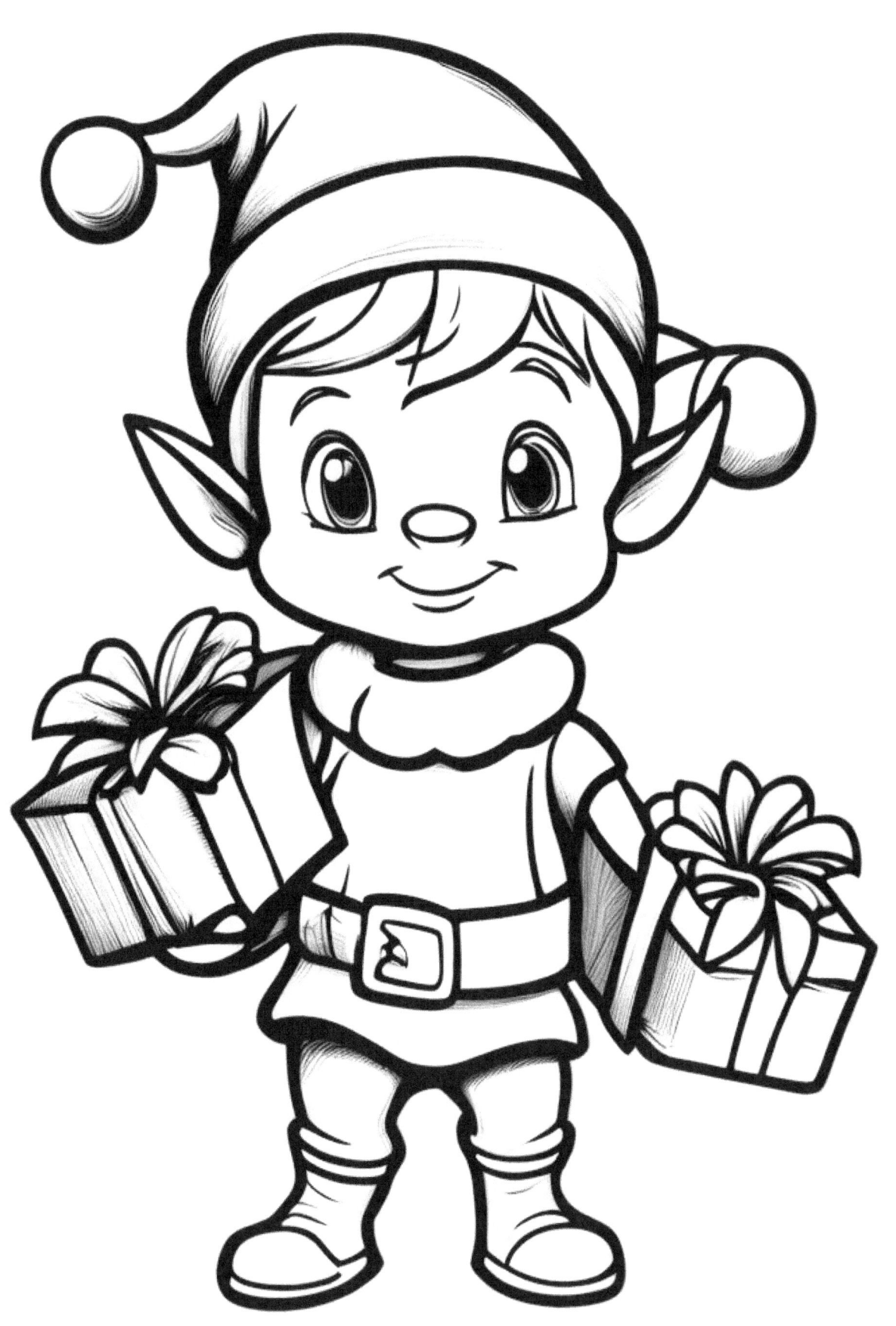

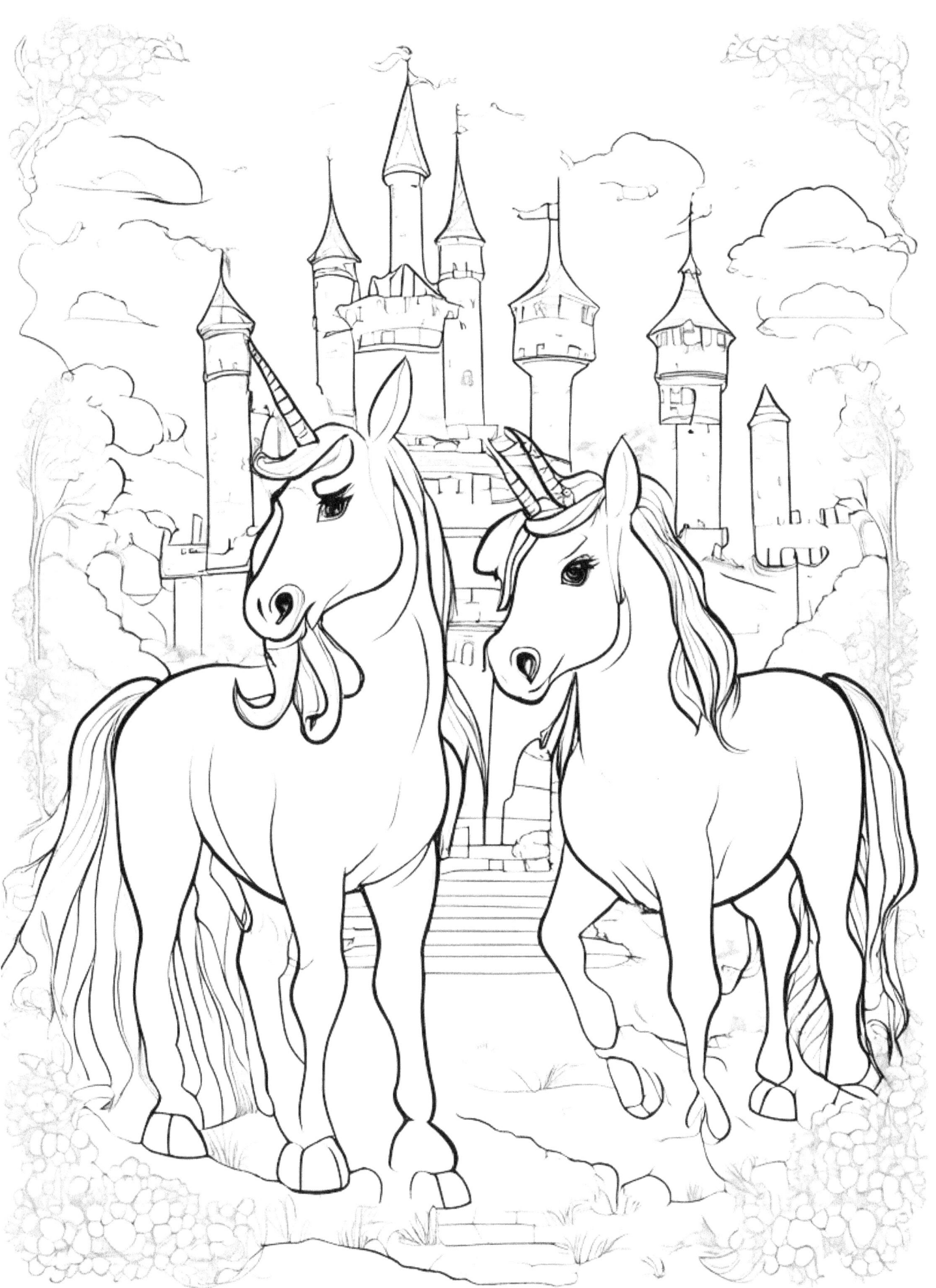

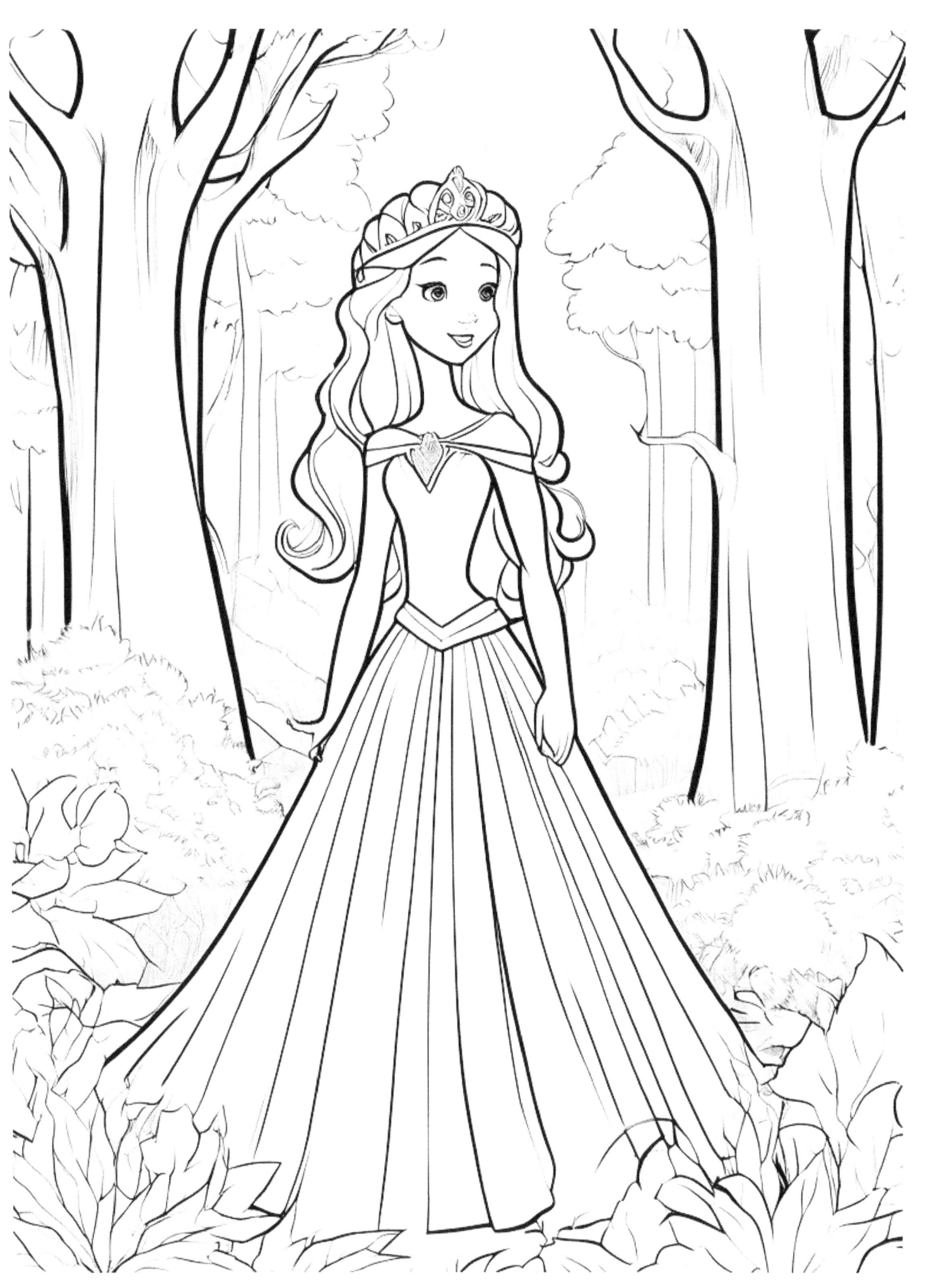

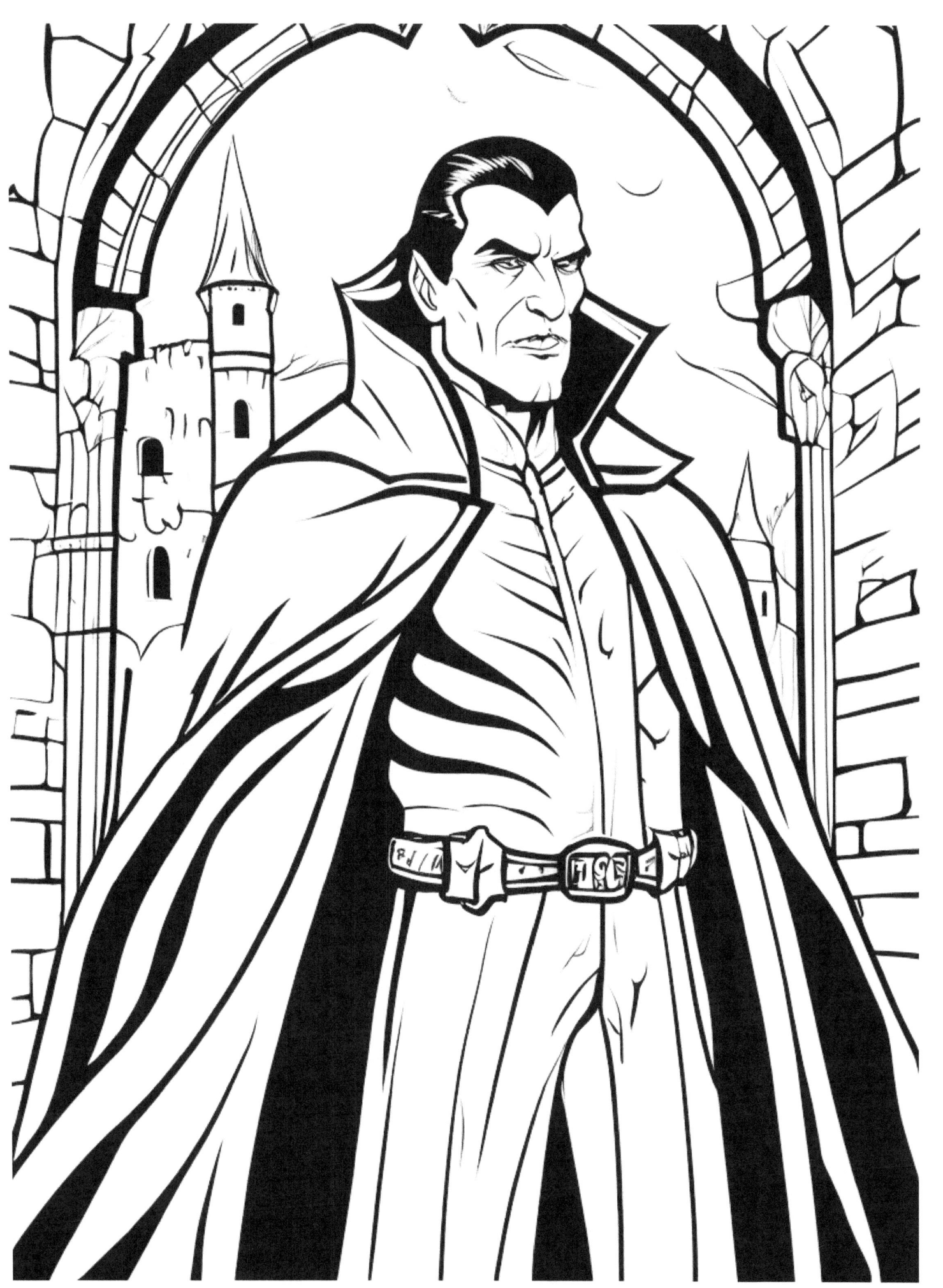

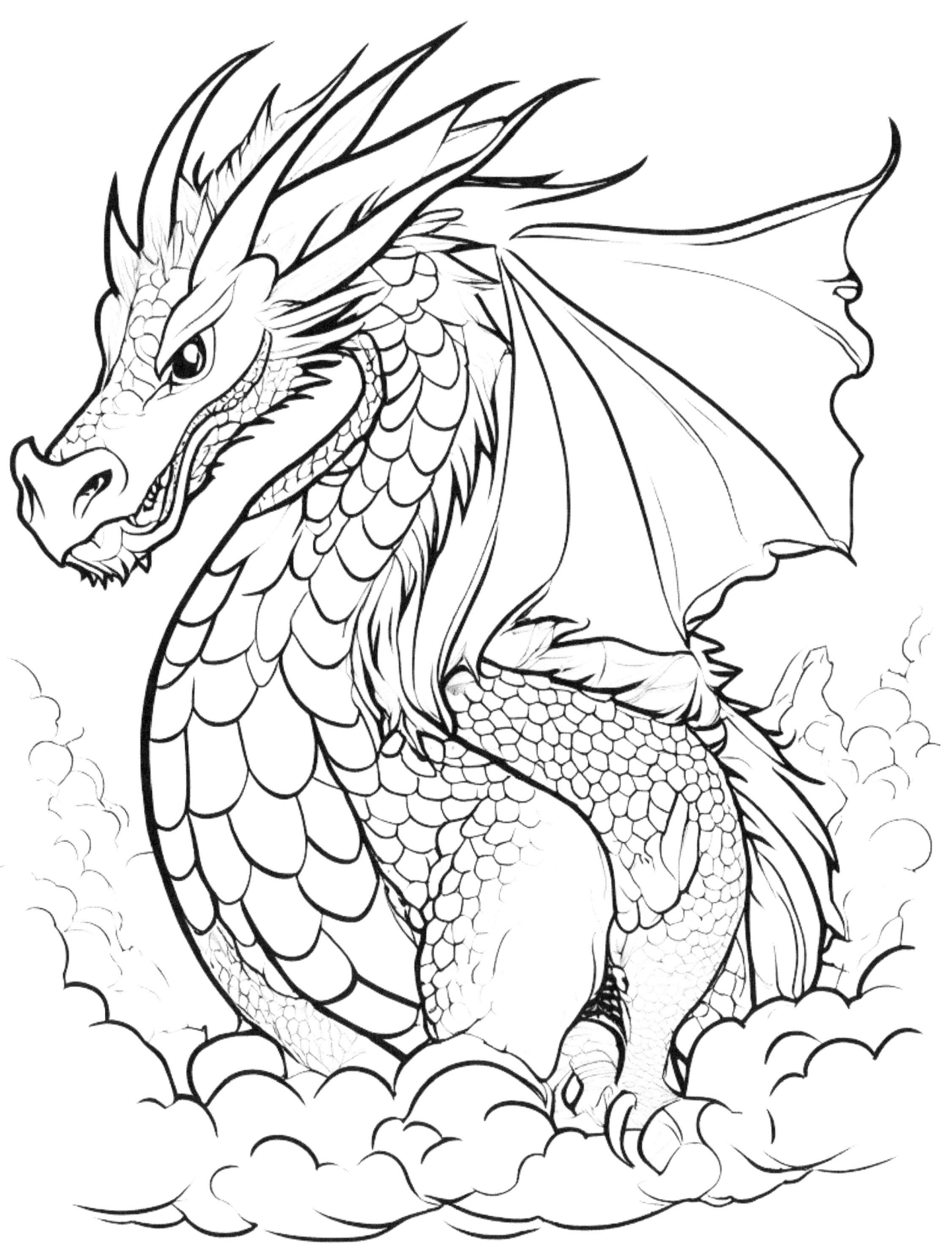

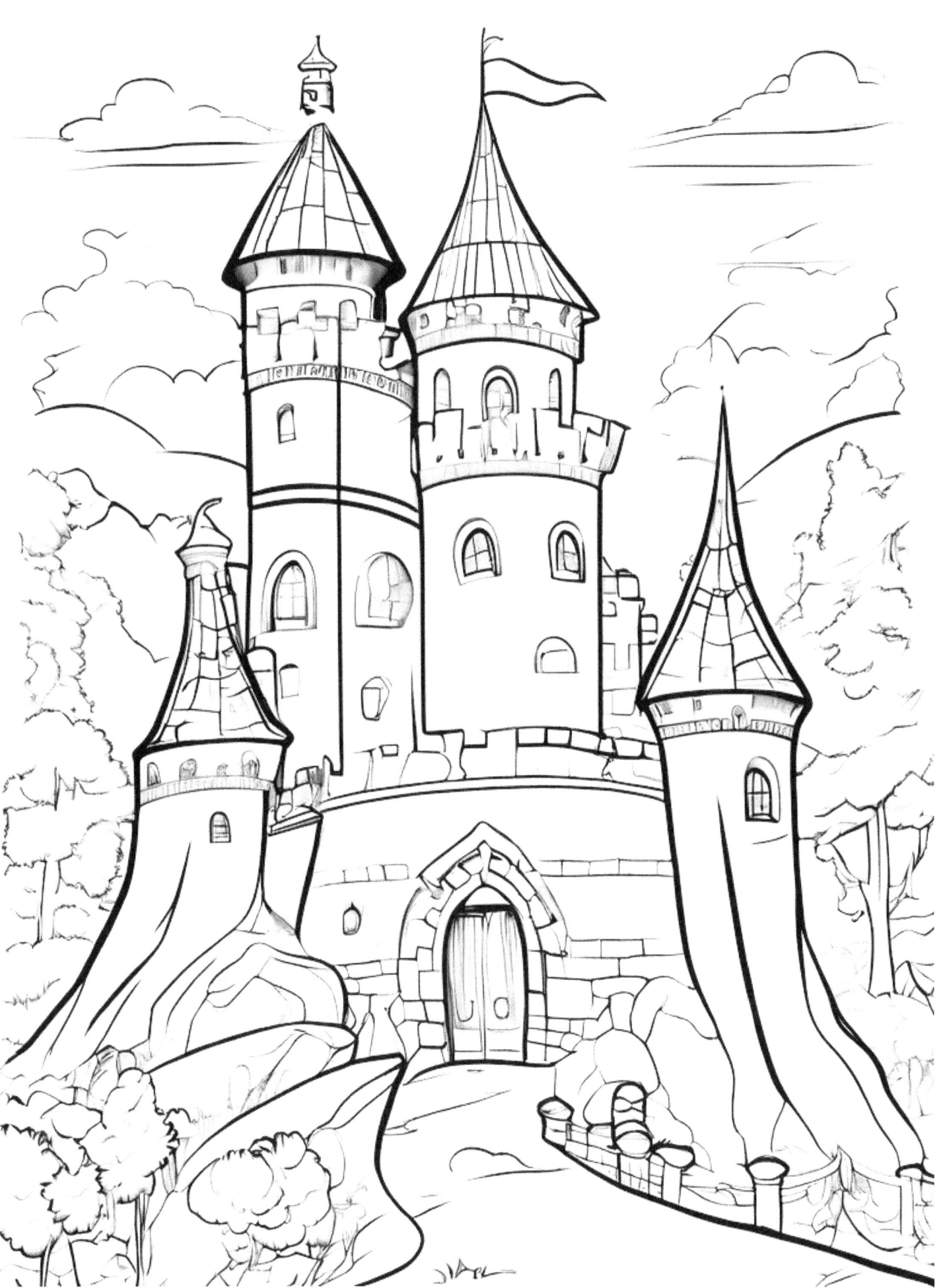

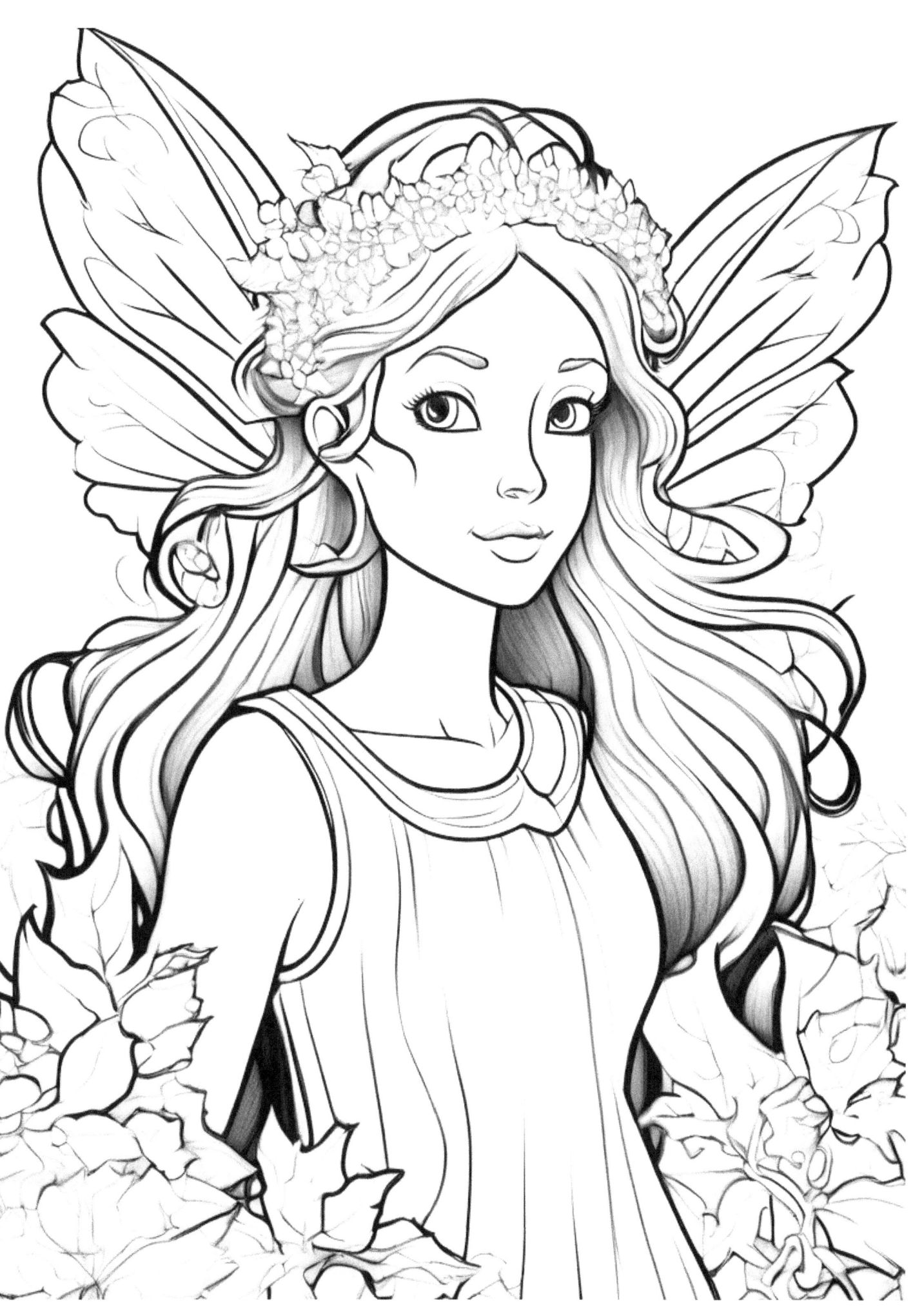

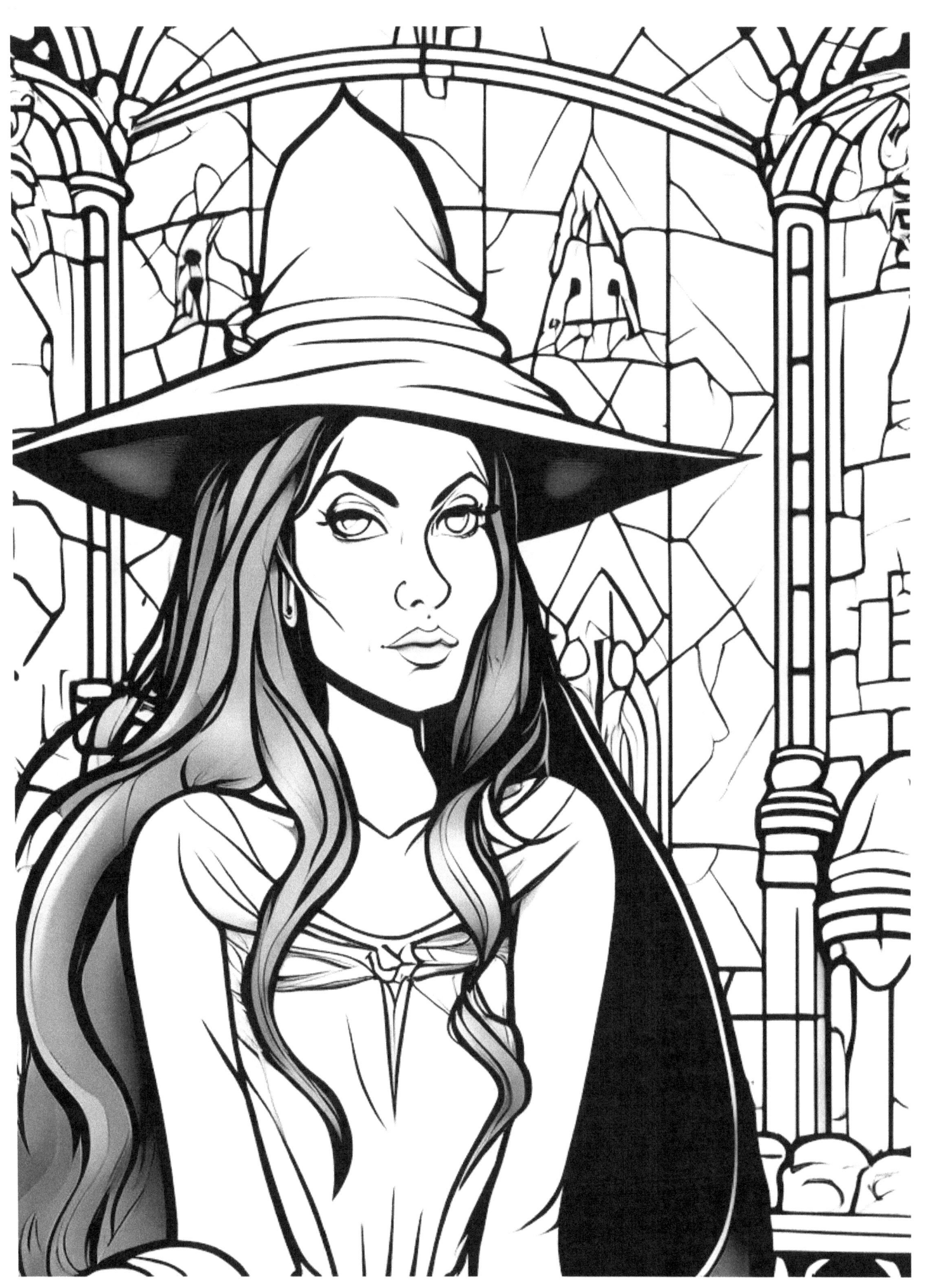

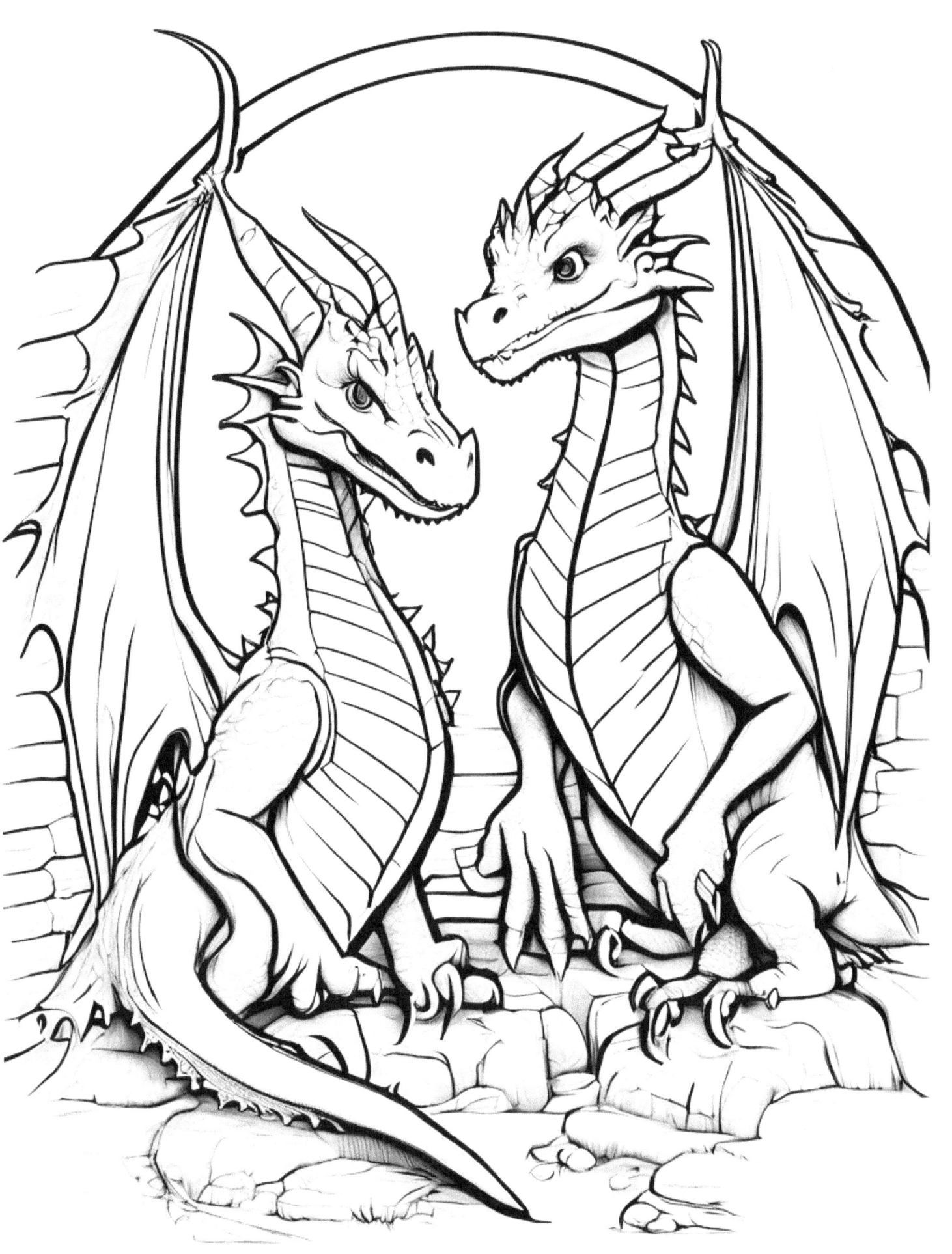

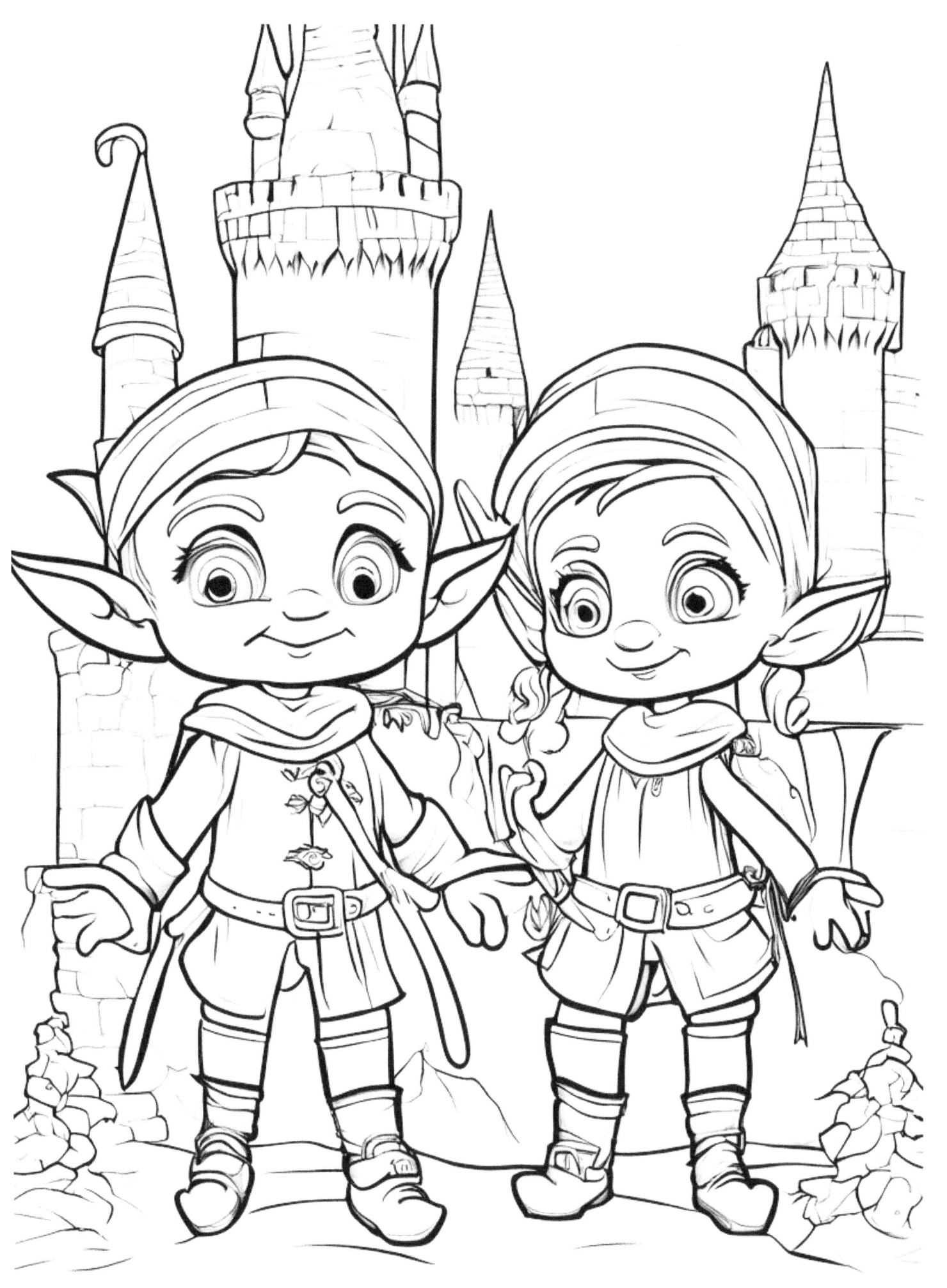

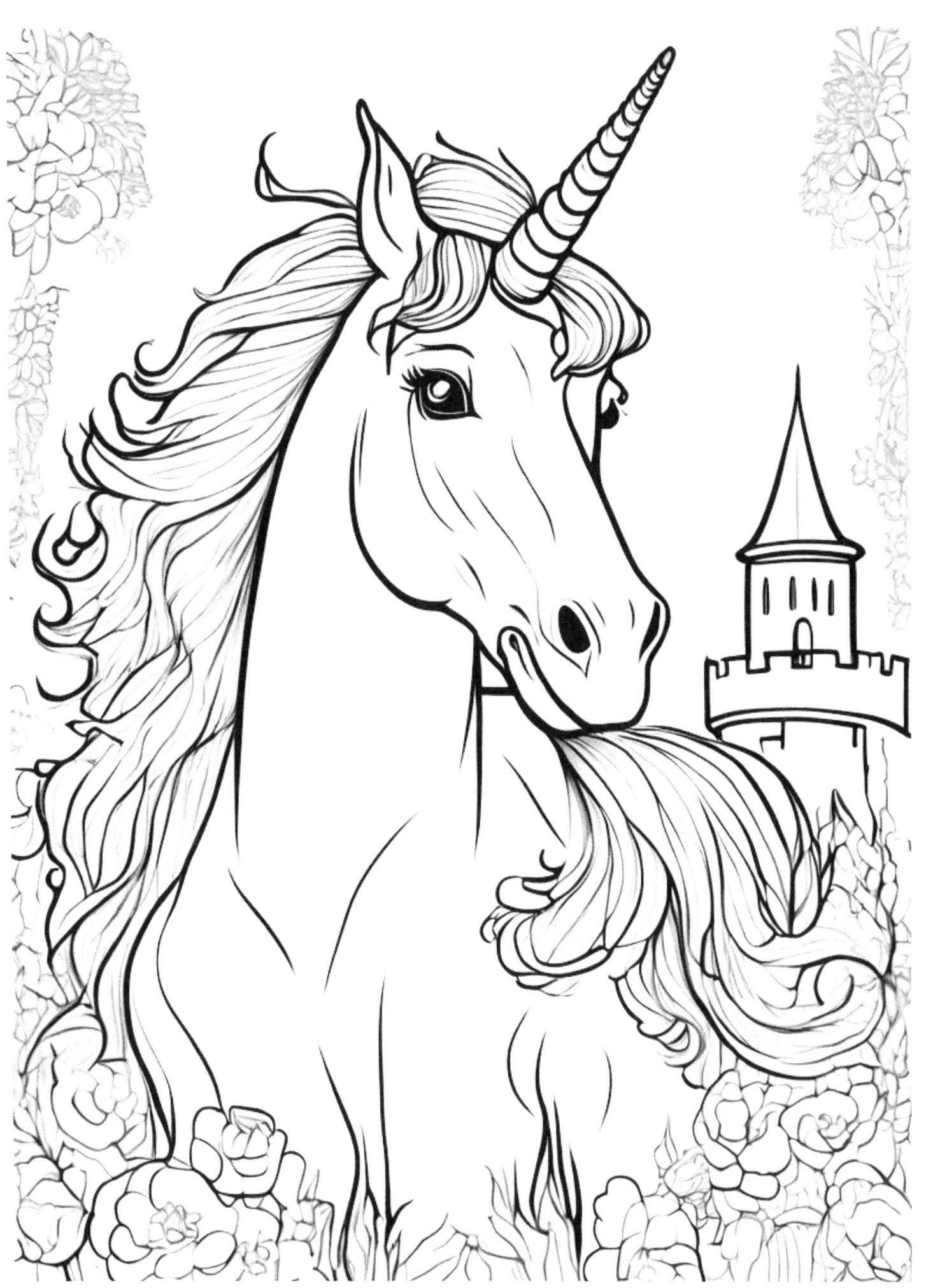

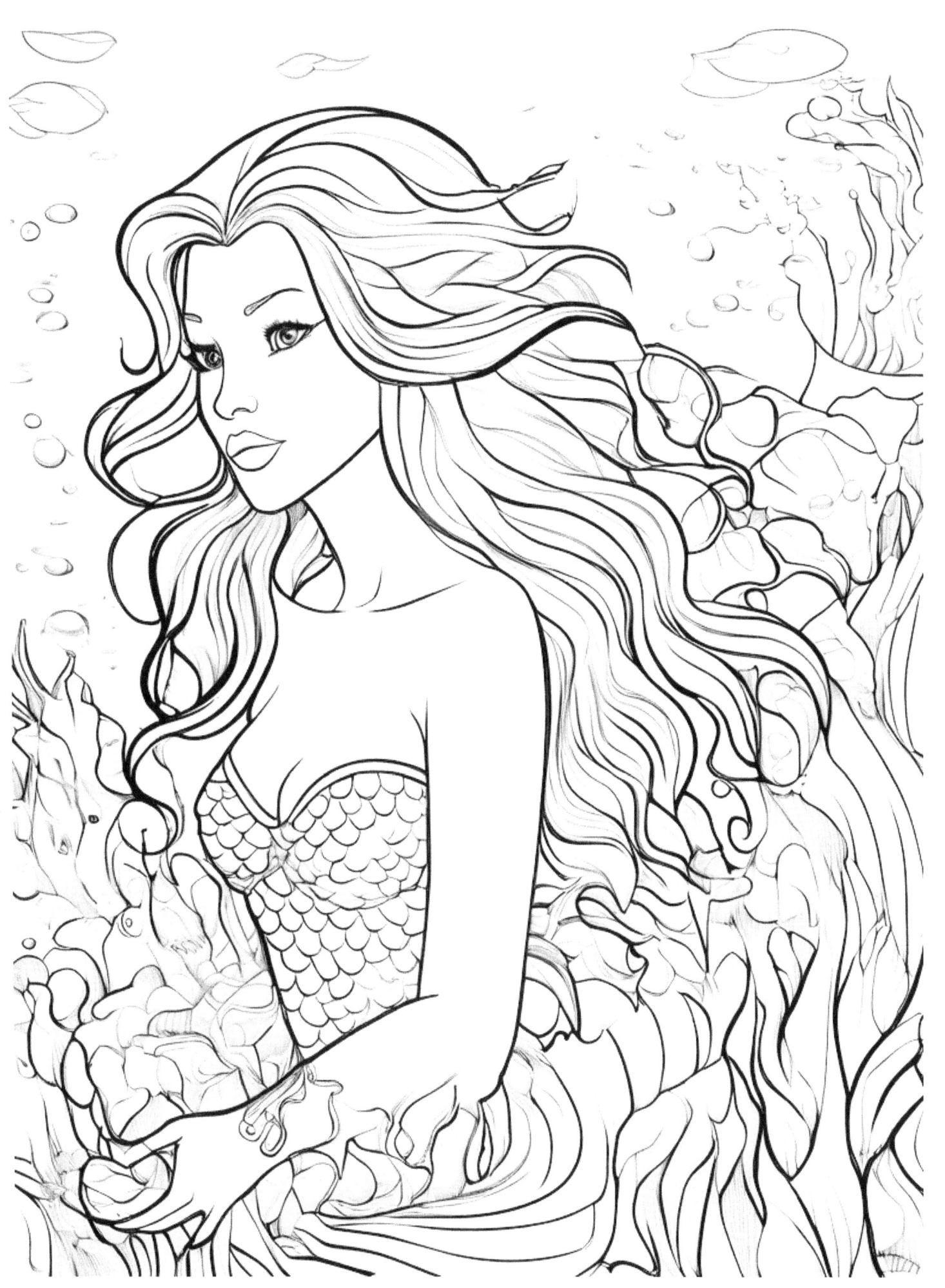

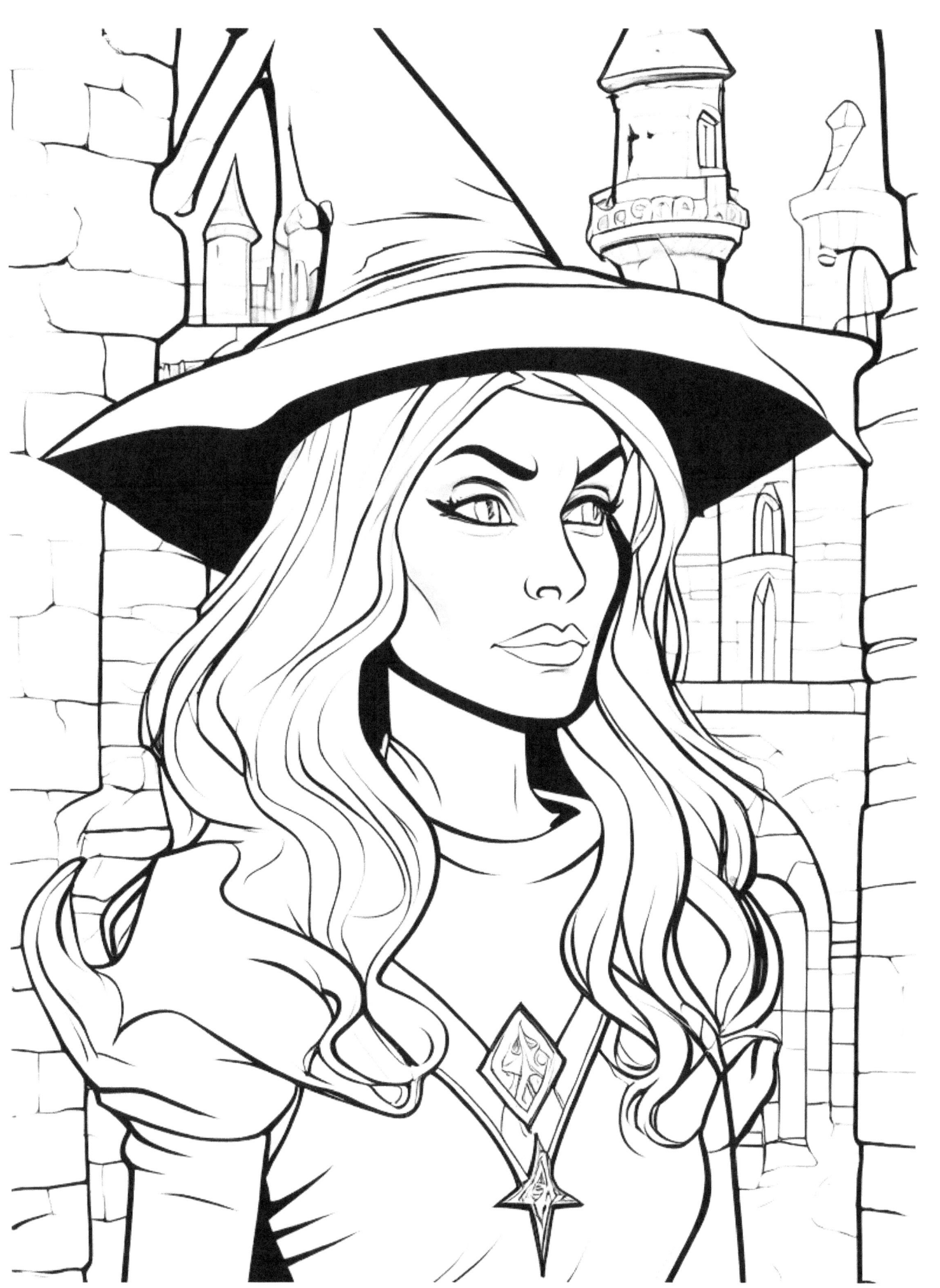

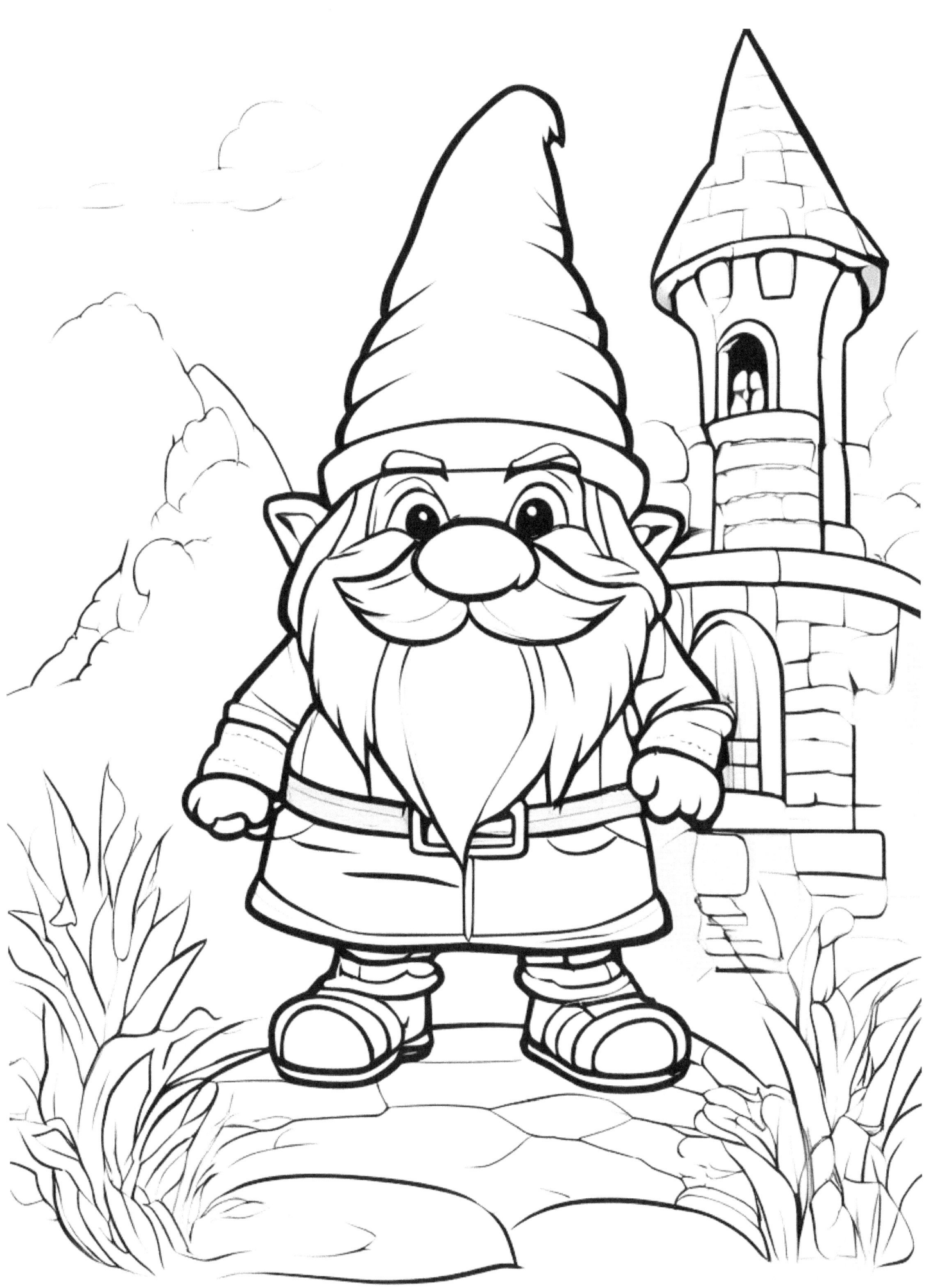

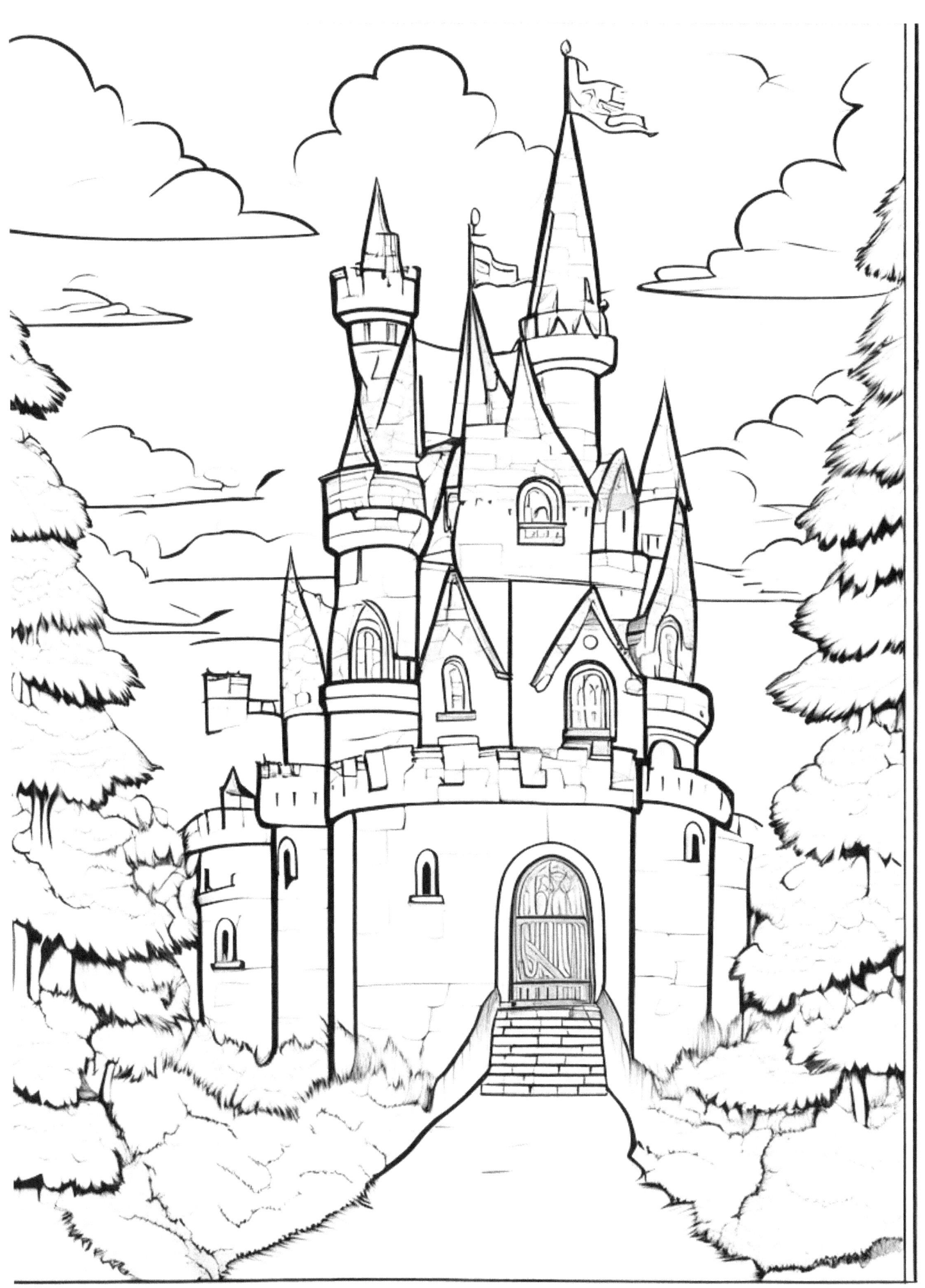

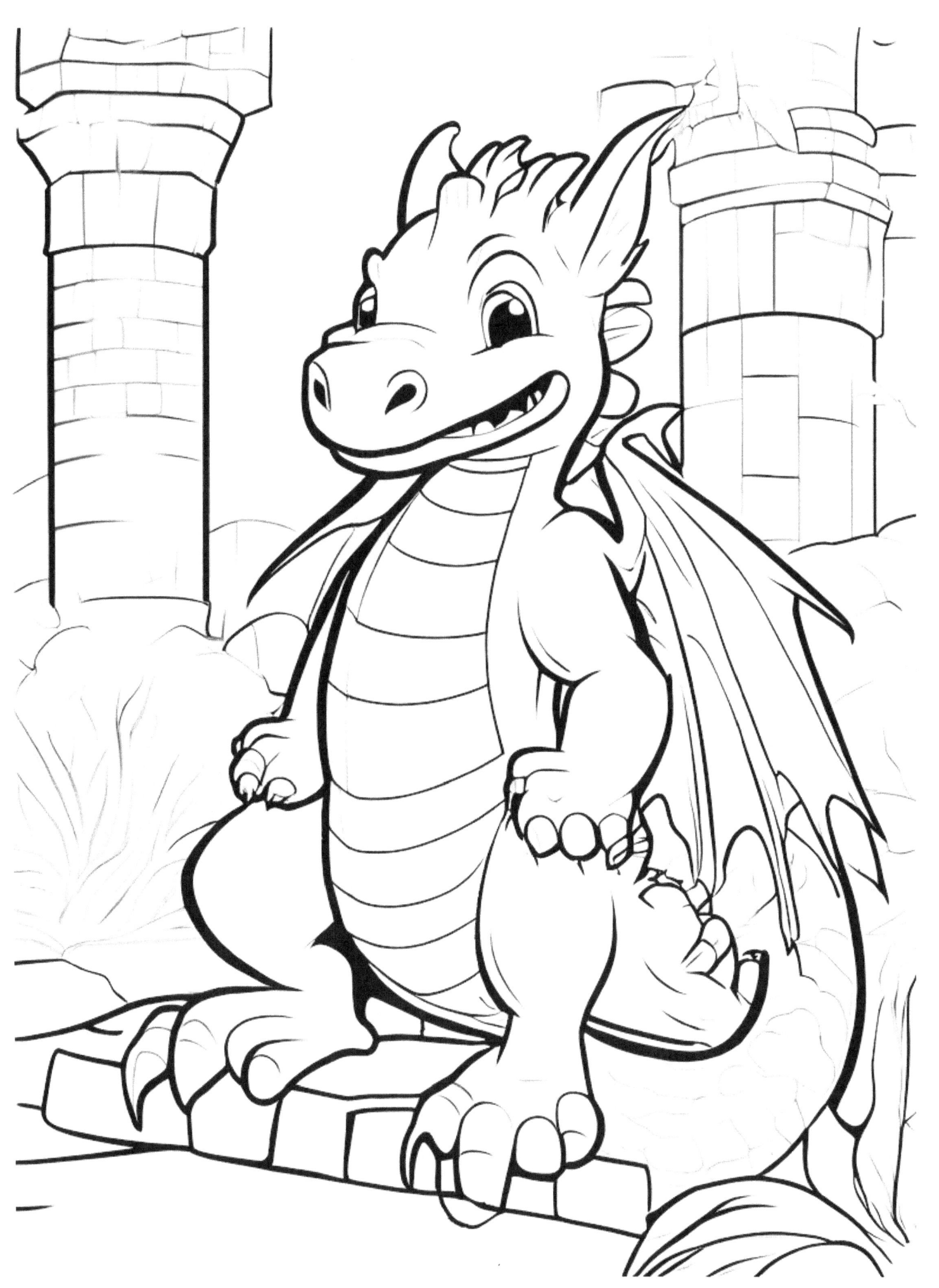

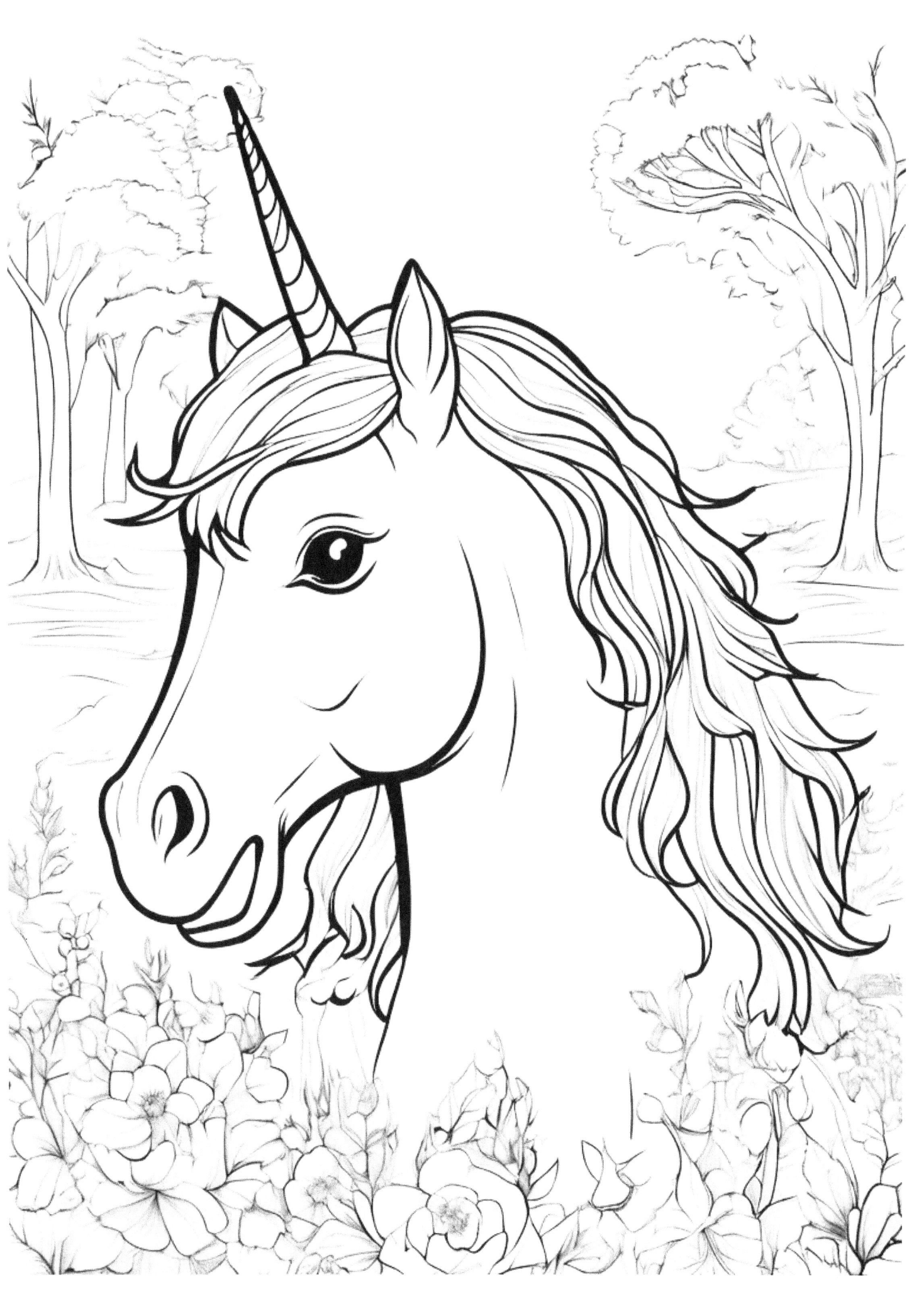

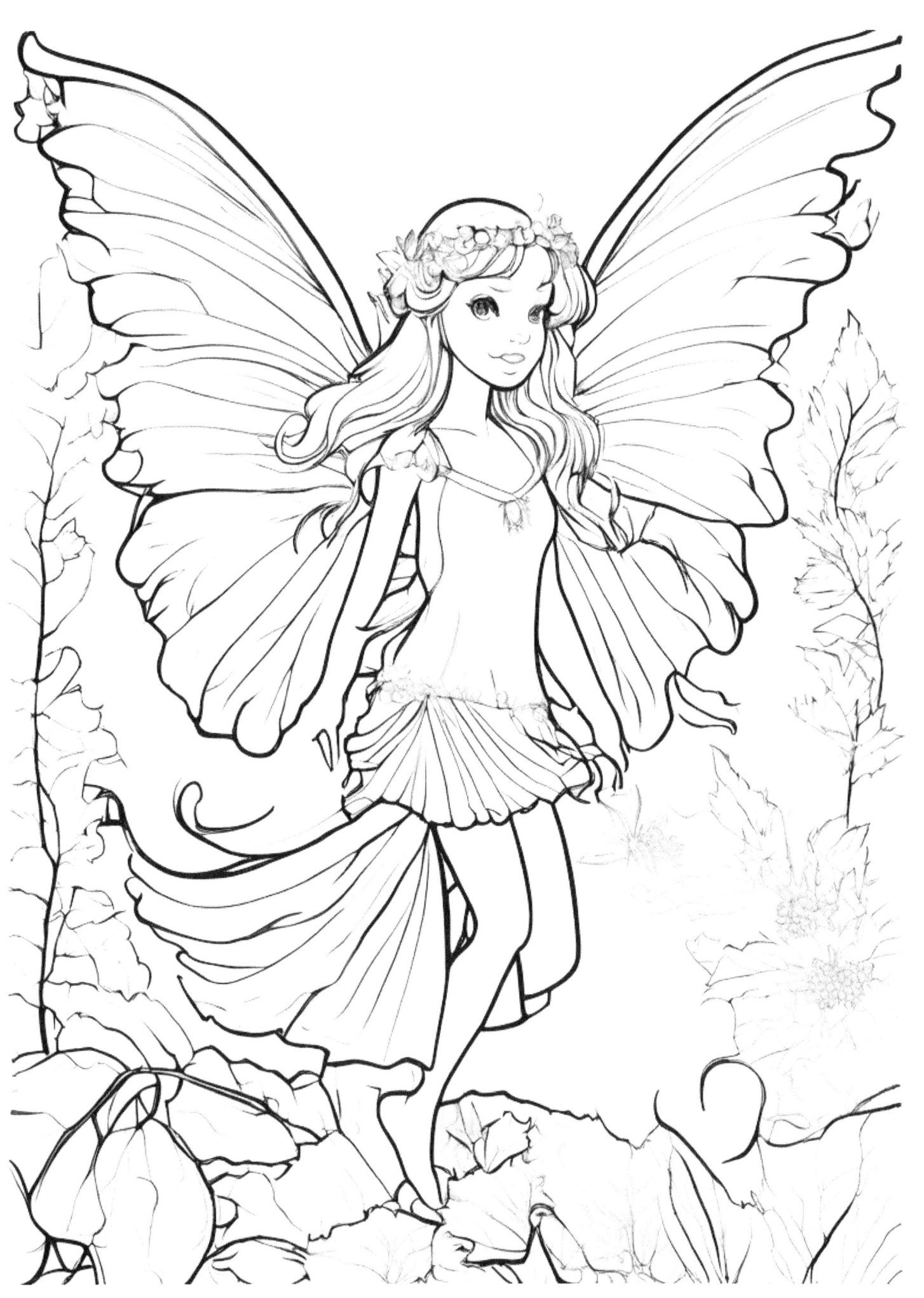

www.ingramcontent.com/pod-product-compliance
Lightning Source LLC
Chambersburg PA
CBHW062118220526
45471CB00010B/3788